MIDDLE-CLASS MILLIONAIRE GOVERNMENT EMPLOYEES

KEY STRATEGIES TO MAKE THE MOST OF YOUR BENEFITS

CLARK A. KENDALL
CFA, AEP®, CFP®
FOUNDER AND CEO OF KENDALL CAPITAL

WITH CAROL L. PETROV, CFP®, CPWA®

www.mascotbooks.com

Middle-Class Millionaire Government Employees:
Key Strategies to Make the Most of Your Benefits

For more information, please contact:
Mascot Books
620 Herndon Parkway, Suite 220
Herndon, VA 20170
info@mascotbooks.com

Library of Congress Control Number: 2023915706

CPSIA Code: PRV0224A

ISBN: 978-1-63755-984-0

Printed in the United States

We are lifelong residents of the greater Washington, DC, area, known as Washingtonians. We have seen firsthand many individuals—including family, neighbors, friends, and clients—who have dedicated their working lives to serving others through public service. We have great admiration for their servant hearts. This book is our small way of "paying it forward" to help those who make our country, states, and communities wonderful places to live, raise families, and grow old.

CONTENTS

Introduction   1

Part I   **3**

Chapter 1: Retirement Planning Since the Roman Legion   5

Chapter 2: Retirement Planning 101: A Baker's Dozen
            Steps to Become a Middle-Class Millionaire   13

Chapter 3: Why Work for the Public Sector?   25

Chapter 4: Examining Your Benefits Deck of Cards and
            Playing Your Cards Right   43

Chapter 5: Benefits from Uncle Sam   61

Part II   **81**

Chapter 6: Beyond Your Pension: TSPs, 403(b)s,
            and 457s   83

Chapter 7: Smart Moves   103

Chapter 8: Common Mistakes to Avoid   117

Chapter 9: Some Things to Think About before
              You Retire   131

Chapter 10: The Many Joys of Government Careers   147

Glossary   155

Acknowledgments   163

About the Authors   165

INTRODUCTION

People are drawn to work for the government for a variety of reasons. They might have a desire to be a teacher, nurse, postal worker, a police officer, or firefighter; to serve in the armed forces; or to do one of dozens of other jobs in the federal, state, or local government.

They might be attracted to the perceived stability or the job security associated with working for the government. They also might feel a calling to do something for the community or the country, in some cases earning less money than they could otherwise but feeling committed to giving to others.

Whatever your reason for working for the government—local, state, or federal—you might appreciate that compared with many private sector jobs, your benefits, including your retirement benefits, are relatively generous. But they can also be complex and difficult to fully understand and appreciate, especially when you begin a job, perhaps early in your career.

Along the way, a government worker will be faced with many choices. The decisions you make can, and probably will, affect you for a long time, particularly if you stay in a government job for years or even decades, as many people do.

Having a myriad of benefits is like being dealt a set of cards. It's up to you how you play those cards. This book is about understanding those cards—those benefits—and making thoughtful and wise decisions on how you play them.

This book is the third in a series on Middle-Class Millionaires. It's about how to use your government retirement and medical benefits wisely while living a financially responsible life. You'll read about how to make smart, beneficial financial decisions, including how to save, spend, invest, and manage your benefits in ways that will help you to achieve lifelong financial security.

This book begins with a general look at retirement planning today, including relevant trends, and provides a high-level overview of retirement planning for government employees.

We then delve more deeply into the retirement benefit options and you. What are your financial concerns? And what are your key benefits? Are you taking full advantage of them? What mistakes do people often make that should be avoided? You might also be in a special situation of some kind. We'll look at some examples that describe the complexity of certain situations and the need for thoughtful decision-making.

How are government benefits evolving? In some cases, because of chronic budgetary constraints, the benefits that you had expected might not fully materialize. What should you do to be prepared for a changing world, one where you might need to take charge of your finances to a greater degree than you had anticipated?

Are you a middle-class millionaire government employee or retiree? Would you like to become one? Please read on.

CLARK A. KENDALL

CFA, AEP®, CFP®
FOUNDER AND CEO OF KENDALL CAPITAL
ROCKVILLE, MARYLAND

PART I

CHAPTER 1
Retirement Planning Since the Roman Legion

The average American baby born today will live roughly 80 years. That's 32 years longer than the life expectancy of Americans born in 1900. People are living much longer and, as a result, having to plan how they'll spend their post-work lives—and plan financially for them. Of course, financial planning takes on greater importance the longer we live.

The notion of retirement and retirement planning is actually quite new. There wasn't much need to think, plan, save, or strategize about how you'd survive financially after your working years were over if you only expected to live to age 50.

There are some records of isolated cases of pensions that predate modern times. In the most famous case, dating back to 13 BC, the Roman emperor Caesar Augustus offered a retirement package to Roman legionnaires who had served 20 years. The payment was provided as an incentive to remain loyal and not rise up against the government.

Fast-forward to 1776, when the new US Congress established pensions for disabled members of the US Army. In the ensuing years, army officers received a life annuity equal to half of their base pay if they remained in service for the duration of the Revolutionary War. And in 1832, surviving Revolutionary War soldiers received a pension equal to their full base pay at the end of the war.

After the Civil War, the US government paid pensions to disabled or impoverished Union veterans or to the widows of soldiers who had died. Similarly, Southern states paid pensions to disabled Confederate veterans. In 1857, New York City created the first pension plan for disabled municipal police officers.

KEY PENSION MILESTONES

Since the mid-nineteenth century, there have been a number of key milestones in the history of pensions, which were designed to acknowledge the sacrifices made by citizens or to encourage people to help build a foundation of education, safety, and protection for our nation. In modern times, however, a government pension isn't considered a gift. It is a financial arrangement whereby a portion of one's salary is set aside and invested in exchange for a promise to receive payments over that person's lifetime.

Here are a dozen highlights, courtesy of the American Society of Pension Professionals & Actuaries:

1875: American Express offers the first private sector pension plan in the US.

1878: New York City establishes a general retirement plan for police officers.

1911: Massachusetts creates the first retirement plan for state employees.

1917: Eighty-five percent of US cities with 100,000 or more people provide some form of pension for their police force.

1919: More than 300 private sector pension plans exist.

1920: The Federal Employees' Retirement Act is passed, providing a pension for all classified civil service employees after age 70 and with at least 15 years' service. Mechanics, letter carriers, and post office clerks are eligible once they reach age 65. Railway clerks qualify for a pension at age 62.

1930: All federal workers have pension benefits; increasingly, state and local government employees do as well.

1930: Twenty-one US states have a retirement plan for their teachers.

1935: The Social Security Act is enacted. In 1935, women are able to begin taking reduced benefits at age 62; in 1961, men are able to do the same.

1974: The Employee Retirement Income Security Act (ERISA) is enacted.

1975: Cost of living adjustments are adopted for Social Security benefits.

1978: The Revenue Act of 1978 adds Section 401(k) to the Internal Revenue Code, and the defined contribution plan is born. The creation of 401(k) plans marked a critical change in retirement savings. The risk and responsibility to provide retirement income shifted from governments—and private businesses—to individuals. This fundamental shift stemmed from the reality that people are living longer than pension actuarial tables predicted. As a result, governments might not be in a position to fulfill their promises forever. Since 1978, governments have reduced their pension promises to new employees. Still, government pension and health insurance benefits are often more generous than those offered within the private sector.

SHIFT IN RESPONSIBILITY FROM EMPLOYERS TO EMPLOYEES

Over the past few decades, the alphabet soup of 401(k), 403(b), and 457(b) plans has radically changed the world of retirement income, transferring responsibility for retirement security from employers to employees—with mixed results.

Instead of being assured of a traditional "defined benefit" pension, which provides a guaranteed retirement income, employees are told, asked, or encouraged to make a "defined contribution" into their own account. Often, their employer will provide a partial matching contribution, but the outcome or ultimate benefit to be received depends on many variables, including:

- How much can or will the individual plan participant contribute to his or her retirement account?

- How is the money invested? Stock funds, for instance, will have much greater growth potential along with more volatility than conservative investment choices.

- How early does the employee begin to contribute to the plan? The earlier you begin to save, the more your account can potentially grow.

- How do the financial markets perform? And how do the individual participant's specific investments perform?

For example, people who retired soon after the global financial crisis in 2009 with a large exposure to stocks were in for a rude and painful awakening. If they panicked and sold stocks or stock mutual funds at a market low, they locked in those painful losses. However, if they were prudent in expecting to retire and had earmarked some of their account to low-risk investments, then they could live off those more stable investments while the markets, and their stock funds, recovered.

LONGER LIVES WITH LESS FINANCIAL SECURITY

In some ways, we've come a long way with our growing awareness of personal financial responsibility and the need for financial planning. However, in many cases and in many ways, we're failing. Americans are living longer and longer, with many more years in retirement, and many of us are less financially prepared to fund those additional years.

In 1940, the life expectancy at age 65 was 12.7 years for a male and 14.7 years for a female.[1] Jump ahead to 2023. The life expectancies for a 65-year-old male and female have risen to 18.4 years and 20.9 years respectively, according to the Social Security Administration.[2] However, their retirement income is less secure for the reasons mentioned above.

Also worth noting, the top-earning 10 percent of Americans live an average of 10 (women) to 12 (men) years longer than the bottom-earning 10 percent.[3] Other top contributors to longevity include education, marital status, exercise, and smoking history.[4]

By retirement, many people have saved only a paltry amount that won't last long. Compounding that problem, almost one in three people choose to take their Social Security benefits at age 62, the earliest age, accepting reduced benefits—30 percent lower, if their full retirement age is 67—for the rest of their lives, when that might not be in their best long-term financial interest.

Given these overall trends, government employees and retirees have generally fared better than those in the private sector, often benefiting from defined benefit pension plans or more generous overall benefits.

But the trends point toward less reliance on a pension and other benefits, with more emphasis on financial self-reliance.

---

[1] Life Expectancy for Social Security, https://www.ssa.gov/history/lifeexpect.html.

[2] Period Life Expectancy—2019 OASDI Trustees Report, www.ssa.gov/oact/TR/2019/lr_5a4.html.

[3] Congressional Research Service: The Growing Gap in Life Expectancy by Income: Recent Evidence and Implications for the Social Security Retirement Age, https://fas.org/sgp/crs/misc/R44846.pdf.

[4] Blueprint Income: How Long Will I Live?, https://www.blueprintincome.com/tools/life-expectancy-calculator-how-long-will-i-live.

Numerous municipalities and states are considering cutting back, or have already reduced, the benefits they had promised their employees/retirees because of pension plan underfunding and financial pressures related to deep budget deficits or possible debt defaults.

The world is changing. We all need to take greater financial responsibility for ourselves, especially when preparing for our senior years. First, understand that Social Security was never meant to be the sole source of income in retirement. Also, accept the reality, whether we like it or not, that state and local governments can and will modify the benefits offered to employees based on tax revenues and their duty to provide for services and infrastructure. It's our individual responsibility to make informed decisions when accepting job opportunities. That's all the more important for every government employee or retiree. That's what this book is all about.

CHAPTER 2

Retirement Planning 101: A Baker's Dozen Steps to Become a Middle-Class Millionaire

This is the one chapter in this book that could stand on its own, apart from the rest of the book. That's because it is general in nature. It doesn't only apply to government employees and retirees. Anyone can benefit from this essential information on how to be financially responsible and achieve financial security. For readers of the first two Middle-Class Millionaire books, this could be a quick refresher course on how to become a middle-class millionaire.

Do you picture government workers as millionaires? Teachers, postal workers, secretaries, police officers, office clerks . . . millionaires? Why not?

If you're not familiar with the concept of a middle-class millionaire, it's simply someone who earns enough money to be considered a member of the "middle class" and who lives a financially responsible life, consistently making wise financial decisions throughout their life as their wealth accumulates. Here's a step-by-step guide on how to become a middle-class millionaire.

1. Spend less than you earn. In other words, live within your means. This is simple, but it takes discipline and a vision. It helps if you establish good daily, weekly, and monthly financial habits and stick with them for the long term. For those habits to become a way of life, they should be anchored in a way of thinking. I call this the "Mindset of a Saver." Simply put, once saving money becomes an ongoing priority, then your wealth will grow.

These financially healthy habits can include creating and following a budget; monitoring your discretionary spending; resolving that you won't try to "keep up with the Joneses" in trying to buy the newest, best, priciest, coolest-looking . . . fill in the blank—smartphone, cappuccino maker, designer jeans, car, boat, vacation home.

Here are some practical, common sense ways to spend less:

- Take care of your vehicle and drive it a few years longer while saving for your next one. With the average cost of a new vehicle at $40,000 or so, why not stretch that cost over a few more years?

- Rent a cottage for two weeks rather than own it year-round. You might pay a few thousand dollars. But think of the money you'll save on the initial purchase, maintenance, insurance, and property taxes by paying only for what you use.

- Send your children to community college rather than a private college.

- Eat out less often. Americans eat an average of 4.2 commercially prepared meals a week.[5] Cut that in half for a while and see how much you might save.

---

5   The Simple Dollar, https://www.thesimpledollar.com/save-money/dont-eat
     -out-as-often.

- Just brewing a daily cup of Starbucks brand coffee at home instead of paying for it at a Starbucks location could save close to $65 a month, or almost $775 a year. That's $7,750 over a decade. Invest that money at a modest 6.5 percent return, and you'll have close to $11,000.[6]

Smart money moves like these can compound and make an enormous difference. Your savings will add up if you do these consistently. It helps to adopt the Saver's Mindset.

2. Save early, save regularly. If you manage to live within your means, then the next step is to save that money. Don't just keep it accessible in your bank account. It will be too tempting to spend it. Officially "save" it in a designated account. It could be for your retirement, your children's college education, a house down payment, or the proverbial "rainy day."

3. Have a clear goal. Whatever you are saving for, make it clear. That simple but critical step will help you focus and visualize what you are saving for, and that will help motivate you and encourage you to add to your savings regularly. Let's say you've been eyeing a Tesla Model 3. It's a beautiful, environmentally friendly car and the most affordable Tesla model. Don't just think about it. Post a picture of it in a room or your office. That could be a powerful and effective reminder to keep saving.

---

[6] "Daily Starbucks Coffee Costs $10,000 Compared to Home Brewing, Consumer Finds," *Milwaukee Journal Sentinel*, March 12, 2014, http://archive.jsonline.com/newswatch/249776901.html.

4. Pay yourself first. This ties in with the steps above. Fortunately, it's very easy for government workers, who typically can contribute automatically to their savings plan through payroll deduction. You can't spend the cash if it gets deducted before your pay goes into your bank account! How much can you save? $100 each pay period? $200? $250? Set it up now, and watch your savings grow.

5. Be prepared for anything. The goal is to create and build an emergency fund that you could rely on in a pinch to pay for three to six months' worth of your living expenses. Being prepared means being ready psychologically and financially for the possibility that you won't have your government job and its various benefits one day. Even if you don't think that seems likely, you just never know. It doesn't hurt to be prepared for anything.

It might seem difficult to create an emergency fund of $40,000 or $50,000. That's not something most people can do without diligently saving. Just begin to save now. Save something every month, and watch your savings grow.

If you save $400 a month ($4,800 a year), after five years, you will have $24,000 saved. If your monthly living expenses are $8,000, that would tide you over for three months with no income.

6. Set long-term goals and monitor them. There's a popular expression: "What gets measured gets done." It's not a guarantee, but how can you reach your goals if you don't have any goals?

What are your financial goals? Put them in writing. Be specific. Consider creating a file folder for each financial goal:

- Your retirement fund

- Your children's college fund

- Your dream vacation

- What else? What are your goals?

You might strive to attain the financial freedom to say, "I quit." Once you exit the working world, your goal might be to purchase a beach house, a sailboat, or a recreational vehicle to live in for a year or two and explore the country.

The key idea is for you to have a thoughtful financial goal that is within your means and is not an impulse purchase that could take years to recover from.

Check on your progress toward that goal every quarter or at least once a year. Keep monitoring your progress, and consider rewarding yourself in some small way every so often for staying on track and making tangible progress. If you don't believe this works, try it.

7. Understand and apply the power of compounding. Compound interest or compound returns on your investments is a simple function of time and your rate of return. The longer your money is invested and the higher your rate of return, the more your money will compound.

There's a simple, powerful, and popular rule of thumb for compounding called "the rule of 72." Divide the number 72 by the annual rate of return on your savings to see how many years it would take for the money to double at that rate of return.

For example:

- If you earn 2 percent a year, your money would take 36 years to double.

- At a 4 percent annual rate of return, your investments would double in half as much time—18 years.

- Double the rate of return again to 8 percent, and it would only take nine years to double.

- And if you were able to earn 12 percent a year, your money would double in just six years. Project that into the future, and see how many times your money could double again and again at a 12 percent annual return. Note: this is an illustration, not a promise of 12 percent annual returns!

This is a powerful example of the value of investing for long-term growth, as long as your money can withstand some inevitable ups and downs along the way. The rule also demonstrates the potential opportunity cost of investing too conservatively if you are saving for a long-term goal, such as retirement in a few decades.

8. Beat inflation. The goal is to grow your purchasing power, rather than see it erode over time. Let's say the price of a quart of milk is $2.50. But with inflation, let's assume the price of milk will rise by 4 percent a year every year for the next quarter century. This is just a hypothetical example. Using the rule of 72 that I just mentioned, you can see that 72 divided by 4 equals 18. The price of milk would double in 18 years, meaning you would pay twice as much for the same carton of milk.

Now, what happens if your money only earns 2 percent while inflation pushes costs 4 percent higher each year? Every year, you would lose more purchasing power. Over time, your dollar would buy less and less milk, bread, or gas. And what if the inflation rate jumps above 6 percent, as it has recently, and stays there? That would erode your purchasing power even more dramatically.

But let's say your money earns 6 percent, and inflation is just 4 percent. In that case, you'd steadily increase your purchasing power over time. With the power of compounding, you would gain more and more purchasing power as time went by. By earning more than the rate of inflation, you could gradually increase your wealth.

To earn higher returns, you do have to accept a certain amount of volatility. That means going beyond keeping your money in low-yielding, lower-volatility savings or investments, such as Treasury securities, bank certificates of deposit, money market funds, or short-term government bonds. Instead, invest in stocks, stock funds, and other higher-growth/long-term investments that have the potential to earn higher returns.

I say "potential" because there are no guarantees. But look back in time—not just over the past year or two but back a century or so. Over periods of decades, stocks have repeatedly outperformed bonds and cash. If you are investing for the long term, it's generally acknowledged that the risks of investing too conservatively will outweigh the risks of short-term volatility associated with stocks.

To have the potential for reasonable investment growth, you need to accept a certain level of volatility. In the investment world, the shorthand for this is that "risk and reward go hand in hand."

9. Understand financial basics and manage them well.
There are two parts to this statement. First, understanding personal finance and managing your money well is essential. If you are financially illiterate and go through life without a basic or sufficient understanding of money, you'll pay the price in many ways. But that's not enough. You need more than just knowledge. You have to be responsible with your money, have your priorities straight, and be disciplined.

That could mean avoiding the latest fad, such as an expensive, trendy new car, or investing in the latest hot stock without doing the proper research and thoughtfully incorporating it into your financial plan.

10. Appreciate and apply dollar-cost averaging. One of the most boring, yet effective, concepts is dollar-cost averaging. It's simple but powerful. You invest the same dollar amount every pay period or month. Let's say $100. Because the price of your investment rises or falls, your regular investment of $100 will buy fewer shares if the price per share has risen or more shares if the price has fallen. Over time, this tends to even out.

Let's look at what happens over the course of three months as the price of XYZ Inc. first falls and then rises. In his first purchase, Ted buys 10 shares at $10 each with his $100. In month two, the price of XYZ stock falls to $8 a share. Ted's $100 goes further, and he's able to purchase 12.5 shares. In month three, the price has rebounded, and it's now $12 a share. Ted's $100 regular investment now will just buy 8.33 shares.

The table below shows that the three-month purchase is 30.83 shares for $300. And let's assume in month four, the price reverts to the original $10 a share. At $10, Ted's 30.83 shares are worth $308.30, even though he invested a total of $300, and the price is back where it was when he started investing.

DATE	PRICE PER SHARE	NUMBER OF SHARES PURCHASED	TOTAL INVESTED	LATEST VALUE
January 1	$10	10	$100	$100.00
February 1	$8	12.5	$100	$180.00
March 1	$12	8.33	$100	$369.96
April 1	$10 latest price—no additional shares purchased	Total: 30.83	Total invested: $300	$308.30

One advantage of dollar-cost averaging is that you buy more shares when the price dips and fewer shares when the price rises. Because of that, you can end up ahead of the game because overall, you'll buy more shares at a discount.

Besides that, there are a few other big advantages to dollar-cost averaging:

- Discipline. You invest regularly. Left to our own devices, how many of us would have that self-discipline?

- Ease. It's automatic. No second-guessing or following human emotions, which all too often guide us poorly.

- No bad timing. It's natural to want to invest after prices rise or to shy away from investing and even to sell after prices fall. But that buy-high/sell-low mentality is exactly how too many investors end up trailing the performance of overall markets. Dollar-cost averaging prevents these costly, emotion-driven mistakes.

11. As an investor, understand and practice diversification. Perhaps the most important advice for investing is to be diversified. It might seem obvious. However, people often are less diversified than they think they are. That's because of duplication within their holdings. Owning 100 stocks or 20 stock funds may not provide actual diversification if many are in the same industry, sector, or region or if they behave similarly under certain market conditions.

Diversification goes beyond the typical asset allocation of 60 percent stock, 30 percent bond, 10 percent cash, which I don't necessarily recommend for everyone. But assuming that classic 60/30/10 allocation is what you want, where is that 60 percent stock allocation invested? Aside from the nine boxes in the Morningstar grid—large/mid-cap/small-cap growth, blend, and value—how much is allocated to developed-market and emerging-market stocks?

How much in large-cap and small-cap international stocks? What about growth and value stocks outside the US as well as within the country?

When it comes to bonds, in addition to government bonds and investment-grade corporate bonds, what about emerging-market bonds as well as high-yield bonds? These can be great diversifiers because they tend to behave quite differently than the more low-yield core bonds. One set of bonds might be exposed to greater interest rate risk, while others are more vulnerable to credit risk in return for higher potential yields.

And what about alternative investments, such as real estate, gold and other precious minerals, commodities, and private equity? These can all have a place in a well-diversified portfolio, though often should represent a small portion, such as 10 percent. Used with discretion, these investments can lower your overall portfolio risk because they often move in opposite directions to the stock market.

Please note that I am intentionally not advocating cryptocurrency because I believe it's too speculative to warrant serious consideration at this time. The performance of Bitcoin and Dogecoin over the past few years, for example, has resembled a trip to a Las Vegas casino. Rolling the dice is not investing in my book.

In summary, when it comes to true diversification, the kind that will limit your losses in a rough market, it pays to delve deeper and more broadly.

12. *Think for yourself, but work with a pro.* I believe that every person has a responsibility to be an informed investor and consumer of financial products and services. Money is too central a part of our lives to relinquish full control to someone else, no matter how much you trust them. However, as you might imagine, from my perspective as a financial advisor, I believe in the benefit most people will receive from consulting with a fiduciary financial advisor.

Fiduciary advisors have an ethical and legal obligation to "do unto others" as they would themselves. You can call it the golden rule of investment advice. Fee-only fiduciary advisors, such as Kendall Capital Management, are only compensated by their clients. That means we receive no incentives to propose one investment type over another.

Again, our personal finances play too large a role in our lives to not attempt to achieve the best results. And to me, that means working with a professional who is doing his or her best for you.

13. Take full advantage of your government benefits. Picture a deck of cards being dealt to every government employee. Are you aware of the cards you've been dealt? Are you playing those cards as knowledgeably and effectively as you can? If not, you could be leaving the proverbial money on the table.

As a government employee, your benefits are important. You might not have taken the job for the benefits, but you are likely aware that they have value. Are you taking full advantage of what they offer? An important part of being a successful government employee or retiree middle-class millionaire is fully understanding and taking advantage of your benefits.

And with that, I encourage you to turn the page and delve more deeply into your benefits. What are they? How much more could you or should you be doing to play those cards better?

CHAPTER 3
Why Work for the Public Sector?

A ll the general information in Chapter 2 also applies to government employees and retirees. That includes living within your means, saving steadily, setting and monitoring goals, and maintaining a diversified portfolio. But let's take a moment to discuss the pros and cons of working for an employer whose mission is to serve the public.

Our society is built on the premise that we should look after each other in key areas of our daily life, such as education and safety. To do so, local, state, and federal governments help ensure these areas are covered. These entities collect income taxes to pay for these services, and, of course, millions of jobs are needed to provide these services. Since governments have a budget and income based on tax revenues, they depend on the community that they serve, and so the public sector faces this additional challenge compared with the private sector.

In the private sector, a company in financial straits can lay off employees. It can also try to sell more goods or provide new services to raise revenues. In the public sector, it's not that easy. Employees generally cannot be fired unless they break laws or are significantly underperforming. Even then, they're more likely to be transferred to a different government job.

However, public employees are often paid less than their private sector counterparts, especially those who play a critical role in making government run smoothly—for example, a civil engineer, scientist, accountant, or attorney. The income disparity can become greater as employees gain education and experience.

There are many possible reasons why people choose a job or career in the public sector. At Kendall Capital, we're not career counselors, but when we help our clients manage their wealth and plan for financial goals, there are many considerations, and they are not always financial.

What's unique for government workers is your extensive menu of benefits. They tend to be more varied than in the private sector, and often you can retain them through retirement. Financial benefits include the pension that the government manages on your behalf, and that includes your mandatory contribution to your defined benefit plan. Some government employees also have a 401(a) plan, which the government contributes to on your behalf and allows you to decide how to invest the money. There are also defined contribution plans called 403(b) and 457(b) plans. These are available to employees who would like to make pretax contributions in addition to their pension contributions. As with the 401(a), participants can decide how to invest the money within the investment company's options, as selected by the government's benefit administrators.

Government workers also have insurance benefits that range from health insurance to life insurance and long-term care insurance. They are all available to employees and their families, often at a subsidized cost and, more importantly, a group rate that's often less expensive than buying coverage on your own. In the case of long-term care insurance, you could secure the coverage while employed and take it with you when you retire. Health insurance premiums will often vary based on the type of coverage chosen.

For government employees, what really matters is years of service. Benefits are negotiated and renegotiated over time. So it's important to understand how long you must work to receive the minimum coverage as a retiree as well as how long you could work to receive an enhanced retiree benefit.

Each state has its own retirement system, with distinct programs for certain subgroups of state employees, such as law enforcement officers, teachers (who often receive a combination of state and county benefits), nurses, doctors, civil engineers, librarians, and university professors. Then there are the employees who simply work for the government to help make it work. Employees within each of these categories may have different benefits available to them, but they have one thing in common: the desire to serve their community and help make it a great place to live. I'm reminded of the cheerful, optimistic, and overachieving character Leslie Knope from the TV show *Parks and Recreation*. It takes a lot of people with that type of civic-minded attitude to make our towns and states places we enjoy.

Then there's the federal government, a popular employer of DC-area residents and provider of jobs around the country in national parks, NASA, the CDC, and numerous military bases, to cite just a few examples. For federal employees, their hire date is also a major factor in their available benefits. People who started working before 1984 are in a different retirement system than those who began on or after January 1, 1984. The old (pre-1984) federal system is called the Civil Service Retirement System (CSRS), and the new system is the Federal Employee Retirement System (FERS). There are detailed explanations of these systems in Chapter 5.

I hesitate to get into too many specifics of federal, state, and local government plans because they are as unique and diverse as the people they employ. You'll find quickly that the more you get into the weeds, the more complicated and confusing this all can seem. With that in mind, I'll stick to generalities and common aspects for now. So, why might someone choose to work for the public sector?

ATTRACTIVE NONRETIREMENT PERKS AND TRADE-OFFS

Schedule. Many are drawn to public service because they place a high priority on a regular schedule. They desire the peace of mind of knowing they can leave their desk at the same time every day and never—or at least less frequently—be asked to work overtime or feel their job is in jeopardy if they can't stay late. This has obvious appeal for parents of small children. Governments know that and use it to entice young, bright people to work for them.

On the flip side, many governments fear a "brain drain" as their employees reach retirement age. Accordingly, they are offering part-time schedules and work-from-home opportunities for some senior-level employees. We have several clients who want to retire but are loyal to their colleagues and don't want to leave them in a lurch. Having this flexibility has helped them ease into retirement while feeling good about sharing their knowledge with their successors.

Income stability. Let's face it, most of us are not wired to take risks and be entrepreneurs or commissioned salespeople. Most want regular paychecks and opportunities to learn and move up the ranks to earn more of that stable income. We're willing to accept modest raises along with years of no raises because the stable income is better than no income. However, recently we've seen several strikes of teachers and nurses across the US and the UK. These frontline workers have endured extraordinary circumstances since the COVID-19 pandemic. Talk with any teacher or nurse you know, and you'll understand why so many walked off the job.

But even before this pandemic, government employees have had their lives changed by regional politics that can decide whether they'll receive a cost of living adjustment (COLA) to allow their incomes to keep up with their increasing expenses. They have also seen reductions in pensions and other benefits. When you choose to work in the public sector, you have to be willing to accept a trade-off: understanding your income and eventual pension benefits are only as good as the union negotiators who represent you and the legislators who you hope are willing to pay you.

THE CHANGING TERRAIN OF STATE EMPLOYEE BENEFITS

An honest, thoughtful discussion of government retirement benefits would be incomplete without including some mention of chronic state budgetary constraints and their impact on employee and retiree benefits programs.

For a few reasons, state retirement benefits programs have been feeling a financial pinch recently. One factor is the demographic bulge created by baby boomers and the significant projected future outlay from various government retirement benefits programs. Compounding this financial strain are ongoing budget deficits, which have prompted state treasurers to look anywhere they can to make up for those deficits and projected financial shortfalls. This is why if you follow in your mother's footsteps and become a teacher in the same county, you will likely have a smaller pension—if you have one at all—and less generous health insurance subsidies. Pensions and retirement benefits are periodically renegotiated. So new employees are offered less in retirement benefits and have to save more on their own.

We won't get into the details of these programs and changes here. Suffice it to say that even when you work for an entity as solid as a government, you just might not receive everything that you had counted on during your career. Where does that leave you? Behind the driver's seat when it comes to taking care of your future through smart, responsible, thoughtful, and diligent actions with the hand of retirement benefits you've been dealt.

STUDENT LOAN FORGIVENESS

The US Department of Education offers a program called Public Service Loan Forgiveness. It forgives the remaining balance on direct loans after an individual makes 120 qualifying monthly payments while working full-time for a qualifying employer. Those employers include federal, state, local, or tribal governments, as well as the military. They also include nonprofit organizations and AmeriCorps or Peace Corps. This program has been around for a few years but initially was overly complicated, and most applicants who tried to apply for this forgiveness were turned down. Fortunately, US Congress has addressed these issues and made it more accessible, so if you were turned down in the past, you're encouraged to apply again. If you work for a government or nonprofit association and have direct student loans, you should look into this program at www.studentaid.gov.

Learn the rules of the benefits card game—and play it well. Your retirement benefits plan documents are not exactly *New York Times* best-selling page-turners. They won't leave you on the edge of your seat. They're fairly dry, detailed documents, but understanding them and making smart decisions about them is vitally important. Over the course of a lifetime, tens of thousands of dollars or more could be at stake if you make poor decisions.

With that in mind: *Make sure you understand the rules of the retirement benefits card game.* Once you understand your benefits, make the most of the set of cards that you are dealt.

Take the time to understand your benefits package, the various options you have, and the choices that you will face throughout your career. Sure, the benefits descriptions might actually put you to sleep. If so, brew yourself some good strong coffee and plow through them. Consider it a smart investment in your financial future.

Typically, people pay little attention to their benefits when they start a job. Fresh out of school, they might simply be thrilled to be earning money. Perhaps they're eager to pay off student debt or to save for a down payment on their first house. Planning for retirement three or four decades away might seem to be a low priority.

Another explanation for early career indifference to work-related benefits is that many people start a job thinking they'll move on after a couple of years. Funny how we hear those stories from people who are about to retire from the government job they've had for three or four decades.

I'll relate the story of a recent retiree, Paul, a classic middle-class millionaire. By nature financially responsible, which he credits to his accountant father, Paul took full advantage of his retirement benefits, always contributing to the Thrift Savings Plan (TSP). In recent years, he has tried to pass those values on to his own son, who now works as a university professor in Chicago. Imagine Paul's frustration when his son, Chris, pushed him away every time he brought up the topic. To borrow from a common saying, "You can lead a son to his 403(b)'s pool of choices, but you can't make him drink."

One goal of this book is to help the many "Pauls" I know help their children to make good decisions about their future and take timely actions.

Once you know what your benefits are and the key choices you'll have to make, think about what makes the most sense for you and your situation, and then make the wisest choices.

For example, when given the option to participate in a defined contribution plan of any kind, try to find the money and contribute generously to your future self. Through payroll deduction, you can make it automatic. The money will go straight into your retirement plan every time you receive your pay. That's called "paying yourself first." It's incredibly effective. Start with that mindset, and it will become a habit, and then it will be second nature throughout your career.

LONG-TERM INVESTMENTS HAVE TIME TO GROW

Aside from "just" participating in an optional workplace plan, choosing the optimal investments for the long term can make an enormous difference over time. So when given a choice of investing more for growth or for short-term safety of principal, remember that your retirement plan is a long-term investment. That means that market ups and downs that might feel rough in the moment get smoothed out over the length of your career. Remind yourself that when the market is down, those mutual funds are cheaper. So the dollars that come out of your paycheck will buy more shares of those funds than they do when markets are up. When the market recovers, you'll be glad you kept on buying those shares. That's called dollar-cost averaging.

Other key decisions, which we'll discuss in the coming chapters, include the following choices:

- When to retire,

- When to take your Social Security benefits,

- Whether to annuitize your investments and how best to do it, and

- How to navigate the various government employee health benefit programs, including the Federal Employees Health Benefits (FEHB) program, and various state benefits.

A TALE OF TWO COUPLES: PLAY YOUR CARDS WELL

To illustrate the potential benefit of playing your cards well, here's a story of two couples, both clients, one with government benefits and the other with a successful business.

George and Ann were both 58 years old. George had served in the army for more than 20 years. He retired seven years ago with an army pension of roughly $110,000 per year and annual veteran benefits of $43,500 tax-free. George then went on to work for the US Department of Homeland Security. Even though George would not receive a pension from DHS, he did start contributing to Social Security, and we projected his annual benefits would be approximately $40,600 at his full retirement age of 67.

Because Ann had been married to George for more than 10 years, her Social Security benefits would be half of George's benefits. That means she could expect to receive about $20,300 annually at her full retirement age of 67.

George and Ann's total estimated benefits at full retirement would be more than $214,000 annually, indexed for inflation. That is more than $17,600 per month. George and Ann, your classic middle-class millionaires, had already saved more than $500,000 in their combined retirement accounts. When we provided them with our estimate for their retirement income, they agreed to invest their retirement funds for long-term growth as potential future "dream expenses" or as assets to eventually pass on to their children or future grandchildren.

Meanwhile, another couple, Rick and Susan, ages 62 and 59, owned three dry cleaning stores. They sold the three stores for $4.5 million last year and netted $3 million after paying federal, state, and local capital gains and income taxes. They expect their Social Security retirement benefits to be $36,000 and $24,000 per year at full retirement age. But unlike George and Ann, they will need to find and pay for health insurance until they turn 65, when they can apply for Medicare.

Rick and Susan can invest their $3 million in a staggered bond portfolio of US Treasury and agency securities (same credit risk) and earn an estimated 4 percent annual return for a total expected annual income of $120,000 ($3 million times 4 percent) while paying for private health insurance until age 65. Then, at age 67, they will receive an additional combined $60,000 from Social Security for a total annual retirement income of $180,000. Not bad.

Why do I tell the story of the small business owner in a financial book on government workers and their benefits? It highlights the fact that these successful small business owners will have retirement income of roughly $35,000 less than a smart, hardworking former employee of the military and a federal agency. It's all about how you play the cards you are dealt.

YOUR PATH, YOUR DECISIONS, AND THIS BOOK

Here's a final thought before you turn the page and delve into the section, "The Deck of Cards," in which we'll get into more detail about benefits and your decisions.

Government employee health and retirement benefits tend to be quite generous relative to the private sector. However, they are also generally more complex. That's why I decided to write this book. That's why it's worth your time to read and review it. And that's also why it makes sense to work with a professional advisor who knows the rules of the card game and can guide you well so that you can make the most of a winning hand.

WHY OUR CLIENTS CHOSE GOVERNMENT JOBS AND HOW THEY BENEFITED

Before we move on to the next chapter, let's hear from a few of our clients about why they chose government jobs and how they have benefited from it.

Helping kids with intellectual disabilities. Lisa, a Kendall Capital client who is married with two children, said she never saw herself working for the government or being a civil servant until that became her career path, and she has no regrets.

While in high school, she and a friend volunteered with the Red Cross one day a week at a summer school program for students with intellectual disabilities. "I loved it," she said. "I just found it fulfilling. I worked with all the ages from kindergarten to college and observed the different styles of various teachers, learning which ones I liked best. My career path was determined that summer."

Lisa has spent her career working in public schools. Back when she was in high school, few people with intellectual disabilities were even allowed to be a part of the educational system. That changed in November 1975, when President Gerald Ford signed into law the Education for All Handicapped Children Act (EHA). The EHA guaranteed a free, appropriate public education, or FAPE, to all children with a disability in every state and locality across the country.

"At that age, my financial future didn't really enter into my thoughts or planning, except I needed a way to support myself. I began teaching in Kentucky and then in West Virginia before returning home to Montgomery County. Neither Kentucky nor West Virginia had as good pension and retirement support as we do here. Once back here, it was an easy choice to begin payroll deductions for retirement to supplement the pension system.

"Any time that I thought about possibly leaving for a private sector job, I realized it would have been for less bureaucracy. But I chose to stay because of the retirement benefits I would lose if I left too soon. My son, who now works for the county school system, may put in his 30 years and then pursue a second career doing something else for a while."

Flexibility to be there for her children. Naomi, a mother of three children, stumbled into her new career in her local school system when she realized she couldn't return to her previous career in the nonprofit sector. As a good middle-class millionaire, she values her retirement benefits as well as the flexibility of a part-time job at her local elementary school.

Her career began with a decade-long stint at the Brookings Institution, a private, nonprofit public policy organization in Washington, DC. She left the organization to stay home with her children. After taking about 10 years off, she was ready to return but quickly learned that "jobs had evolved," she said.

"New skills were needed, and I didn't want a long commute. So, when I was asked if I would be interested in a part-time job at my children's elementary school, it seemed to be a great way to transition back into the working world.

"The school system can be an ideal workplace for people with school-age children," she said. "Summers off, with holidays and snow days that are in tandem with your children's schedule. Many of my part-time colleagues in the school system work there mainly because of the health care benefits. I have colleagues whose spouses are realtors, small business owners, and law firm partners, and my colleagues all carry the health care benefits for their families.

"Little did I know that a small part-time position would turn into a rewarding 20-year second career for me. I went back to school to obtain the necessary credentials to work as a professional media specialist in the school system. Montgomery County Public Schools offer many opportunities, such as the ability to work in different schools, training, and partnerships with local universities for advanced degrees in different subject areas."

Most teachers stay with one school system for their entire career. Unless you transfer to another school system early in your career, you don't get credit for your years of teaching at the first job and usually have to start at a lower salary level.

There is not much movement from private schools to public school or vice versa.

"As I get closer to retirement," Naomi said, "I find it is important to pay close attention to the retirement guidelines, especially concerning health care and leave payout. The amount of the employer's contribution for retirement health care is based on years of service. Some of my colleagues are working a few years longer than expected so they can receive a higher employer contribution. If you notify human resources by a certain date, an extra amount of sick leave is paid out. Fortunately, there are seminars and lots of resources available to help people make the best decision for their situation."

"I pursued the job because I like helping people." Ellen is recently divorced, with no children. She has come to deeply value her pension after working for more than 30 years in the public school system. She works in administration, which can be a thankless job. However, without administrators coordinating and communicating with many interested parties— including county council, parents, and teachers—there'd be no school system at all.

"I was inspired to become a teacher when I learned about teaching strategies that can truly help students to learn, and I realized that I would have learned more than I did had I been taught using those strategies. In my day, school was about memorization and rote learning whereas real teaching can be hands on with connections to real life. I also personally experienced and observed mistreatment—of me, toward my parents, or involving a relative due to misperceptions or misunderstandings. So I wanted to do a better job supporting students and their families, given my own experiences. I also wanted to be an advocate for doing the right thing in support of kids when parents don't have the financial resources.

"Money never really has mattered to me. I pursued the job because I love helping people. I did not even know there was a pension or understand what a pension is, but now I greatly appreciate that I have one. I thought about my future financial security before I got married, then got sidetracked, but now I am back on my feet. My divorce really got me to think hard about what I need to do for myself instead of being overly generous to others and taken advantage of.

"I always wanted to pursue business management, but in college, I decided that an educator could become a business person more easily than a business person could become an educator, so while I could have tried to transfer into Wharton while at the University of Pennsylvania, I pursued a degree in education instead. Whether or not that was a smart move, I will never know, but I know passion drives people, and I have done well for myself pursuing my passions. While I have been offered several opportunities to follow people who have become superintendents elsewhere, the offers were never enticing enough for me to actually want to pursue them."

A mix of tangible and intangible benefits. When Bob returned from serving in the army during the Vietnam War, he had a college degree, but he realized that to land a job, he needed more marketable skills than knowing how to jump out of airplanes. So he learned more practical skills, including typing, and took a job with US Customs and Border Protection, thinking that it might lead to travel opportunities. His ultimate dream was to work as a diplomat and travel the globe. Unfortunately, while he had the skills, the political timing wasn't right.

"However, I embraced the chance to travel across the US, and I made friends all around the country in my 35-year career. I'm a people person, so I loved my work in human resources and training. I was also on the pioneer front, digitizing records on some of the first computers in the federal government. I truly valued being able to earn a stable income and having time to spend helping to raise my three daughters since my wife also worked full time at a state university."

Bob and his wife, Anne, whose story appears next, appreciate their pensions but also saved in their retirement plan accounts, allowing them to enjoy exciting international travel now that they are retired—typical middle-class millionaires.

Free college education—a smart move. Anne worked at the University of Maryland for 42 years. She saw a number of practical benefits, including great work-life balance and other perks that come with being university staff.

"I chose UM as an employer because I wanted to go to school, and I knew the benefits were good," said Anne. "I ended up getting two degrees for free, and all three of my children got tuition remission for undergraduate work.

"I had many different jobs at the university. Whenever I got restless or didn't like my boss, it was easy to change departments/jobs and still keep all my benefits and seniority. When I needed to, I found a part-time job, which was perfect at the time as I needed the flexibility, and I still had benefits."

Because Anne's health insurance through the state of

Maryland was better than her husband Bob's federal government plan, she carried the family's health insurance plan.

"I realized that the good quality of life that came with working there was a good trade-off and was worth earning less money," she said. "For example, if it was a snow day for our girls, it was one for me too. The leave system was generous, allowing me to take plenty of time off. I left when I retired, and it was hard to make that decision because I had a great job."

CHAPTER 4

Examining Your Benefits Deck of Cards and Playing Your Cards Right

This book is about making the most of your government benefits "deck of cards." That means understanding your benefits, taking full advantage of them, and then looking beyond them for additional savings in order to take care of your financial future as a middle-class millionaire.

The keys are to learn about your benefits so that you can follow smart strategies, use time to your advantage, and of course, make wise and thoughtful choices along the way.

This book is intended as a general guide to government benefits, rather than an encyclopedic, all-encompassing reference source. It is primarily focused on retirement and, to a lesser extent, some major insurance-related benefits, such as health, life, and long-term care insurance.

The purpose is to answer broad questions, make general observations and recommendations, and teach some fundamental lessons to help government employees and retirees navigate complex and confusing terrain.

WHAT CARDS HAVE YOU BEEN DEALT?
HOW WILL YOU PLAY THEM?

Do you know what's in your benefits deck of cards? Take some time to read, understand, and consider your best benefits options.

- What are your actual pension plan benefits? When are those pension benefits vested? Are they portable? Or will you lose them if you leave your job?

- How are your retirement benefits calculated? What might your actual pension look like? Will the monthly income you receive be enough to live on? What can you do in case it isn't?

- To ensure that you have enough to live on in retirement, have you considered also saving through other means, such as a 403(b) or 401(a) plan?

- Are you eligible for Social Security benefits? Find this out so that you can avoid any nasty surprises when it could be too late to take corrective measures.

This chapter is largely focused on major benefits-related decisions that you and other government workers will make at key points in your career. To illustrate the choices, we'll use three hypothetical people:

- Steven is 25 and is just starting a government job.

- Mario is 45, in the middle of his career, and is juggling numerous priorities.

- Becky is 60 and is doing detailed preretirement planning.

STEVEN'S KEY EARLY CAREER BENEFITS DECISIONS

As a recently hired municipal government employee, Steven goes through an orientation process, where a human resources counselor explains his compensation and benefits package to him. Steven has to absorb a lot of benefits information while he learns all about his job responsibilities. Fortunately, with some automatic defaults, this is an easier process than it used to be, but the onus is on Steven—as it is with each of us—to understand his benefits and make wise choices. The days of relying on a benevolent, paternalistic employer to watch over us are long, long gone.

THE THREE-LEGGED STOOL

As a newly hired civil engineer, Steven is enrolled in the pension plan of his employer, the city of Baltimore. He will also contribute to Social Security through payroll taxes and enjoy Social Security benefits when he retires. And he will have the opportunity to save through an employer-sponsored 401(a) plan, which is like a 401(k) plan for some government workers.

STEVEN'S KEY RETIREMENT BENEFITS CHOICES

The pension plan and Social Security benefits are automatic, guaranteed benefits to which Steven and his fellow employees are entitled.

The 401(a) plan differs in that there are various options. Although certain choices are made automatically for plan participants in some plans—for example, the enrollment, contribution amount, and choice of where to invest the money—Steven could override those selections. For example, if he really didn't want to save for his future, he could opt out of contributing anything. Very few employees do that, however. After all, who wants to leave free money on the table in the case of a matching employer contribution? He could also decide to contribute more than the automatic deferral amount of his salary, up to an annual maximum set by Congress.

Steven also could choose to invest differently than in the default investment. For example, if his plan automatically places employee plan contributions in a target date fund and he seeks higher potential returns by allocating more of his savings to stocks, he can do so. Conversely, if he prefers a more conservative mix than the plan's defaults, he can go in that divergent direction.

HOW MUCH TO SAVE IN THE 401(A)?

A general rule of thumb when contributing to an employer-sponsored retirement savings plan is to contribute at least enough to capture the full employer matching contribution, if there is one. In this case, Steven is automatically enrolled at a deferral rate of 4 percent of his salary, all of which is matched by his employer. If he is able to save more, that's great, but this early in his career, Steven isn't earning that much, and he has other financial obligations. So he decides to stay at the default contribution rate of 4 percent for now.

However, if you can afford to save even more, why not do so? Steven may have an additional type of plan, such as a 403(b) or 457(b), through his employer. As he is only 25, his salary is still relatively low, so he wouldn't benefit that much from a tax deduction. If he's interested in saving more money, he could open a Roth IRA, where he could invest up to $6,500 per year. We go into more details about the virtues of Roth IRAs in Chapter 6 and how they're particularly versatile and come in handy for the younger savers.

I have met plenty of retirees who have accrued millions of dollars in investments, and I don't recall many of them telling me, "You know, Clark, I should have saved less money!" Instead, they're enjoying their financial security, and they might also be enjoying thinking about the many things they could do with their wealth. Perhaps spend some on vacations, second homes, and gifts for their children and grandchildren. They might give some money to a favorite charity now or leave some for charities in their will. Keep in mind that they wouldn't have those choices now if they hadn't saved the money in the first place.

MARIO'S MIDCAREER REVIEW

Let's meet Mario now. Like Steven, he's a character created to illustrate part of our career life cycle of financial choices. Maybe you can relate to him. At age 45, Midcareer Mario is halfway between 25 and 65, roughly 20 years into his career and 20 years away from retirement. Unlike Steven, though, Mario is employed by his local county school system.

Let's see how Mario is doing on his financial journey and what his benefits choices look like. As with many of us, Mario didn't have a firm goal or target for his retirement when he started out. And unlike Steven, Mario didn't have automated retirement plan features when he began working as a teacher in 2000.

When he began his job, the onus was on Mario to enroll in his 403(b) retirement plan, as well as to decide how much to contribute and what to invest in. Typically, 403(b) and 457(b) plans offer two types of investment products—annuities and mutual funds. The annuities fall under three basic types: fixed, variable, and indexed. The mutual funds are typically stock funds, bond funds, and money market or short-term, cash-like investments.

Mario opted for mutual funds because he found annuities confusing, and he had heard negative things about annuity fees and restrictions. Because he didn't know much about investing, he was apprehensive about being too exposed to market volatility, and back in 2000, the dot-com bubble had just burst. So at first Mario put roughly two-thirds of his money in a diversified bond fund and the other third in a money market fund.

REALLOCATING FOR ADDITIONAL GROWTH

After a few years, Mario began to realize that a retirement account with all of its money allocated in bonds and cash, which was earning less than 5 percent a year overall, was far too conservative for a goal four decades away. He didn't like missing out on the higher potential long-term gains achieved by stock funds. So he changed his new contributions to a much more diversified mix of stock funds and bond funds. His allocation was roughly 60 percent in stocks and 40 percent in bonds and cash. That's a fairly traditional approach, given that the 60 percent stocks/40 percent bonds allocation tends to be a general default or guideline for balanced funds. It's also much better than not owning any stocks at all.

Because Mario doesn't know a lot about investing, a good option for him and for others like him would be to consult with a fiduciary financial advisor, whose unbiased expertise would guide him on his personal finance journey. Although I'm clearly biased, why not receive personal guidance from a financial professional who is legally obligated to put your needs first? We all have individual needs, priorities, situations, and investment personalities. So, why not receive expert, personalized professional assistance?

ROTH OR TRADITIONAL CONTRIBUTIONS?

A Roth option in a retirement account is an important consideration for Mario, as well as anyone else with access to one. Such contributions offer an opportunity for tax diversification. The key difference between a Roth account and a traditional retirement account is that with a traditional account, you get a tax deduction when you contribute to the account, but your withdrawals will be taxed. With a Roth account, you receive no tax deduction when you contribute to the account, but you won't pay any taxes on your withdrawals.

Ideally, you should have a good mix of money in both Roth and traditional accounts so that once you're retired, when you need to withdraw money in any given year, you can decide whether it makes more sense to take taxable or tax-free withdrawals. For example, if taking taxable withdrawals would raise you into a higher tax bracket, maybe that's a good year to take tax-free withdrawals.

INCREASED CONTRIBUTIONS?

Mario should also review whether his retirement savings are on target to meet his goals. If not, perhaps he could increase his contributions to his 403(b) and boost his retirement savings. Mario started low, contributing just 3 percent of his salary, but he later increased that to 5 percent.

Perhaps Mario could boost that even further now. With 20 years of potential earnings growth ahead of him, even increasing his contributions by one or two percentage points could make a meaningful difference over the long term.

After working for 15 years, he has the opportunity to make additional "lifetime" catch-up contributions to his 403(b). These plans have a unique feature that allows a participant to make up to $15,000 in catch-up contributions even before they reach age 50.

While some 403(b) plans offer matching employer contributions, most don't. Instead, the employer may offer a 401(a) plan to which they make matching contributions. If you are eligible to participate in such a plan, it's a smart move to look into it and see if you can take advantage of this additional retirement savings option.

Another option may be a 457(b), which would allow Mario to contribute or defer more of his salary on a pretax basis. Here again, these contributions are not "matched," but if Mario is able to, he could save the maximum amount allowed by the Internal Revenue Service in both the 403(b) and the 457(b). In 2023, that would be $45,000 without including a possible catch-up contribution on the 403(b) if you're 50 or older or any employer matching contributions.

Although that isn't the same as getting a bonus from your employer for saving, it does allow you to give your future self that bonus! And your future self might just thank you for being so thoughtful and generous.

BECKY'S BEST BETS ON RETIREMENT BENEFITS

Now it's time to meet Becky, who is 60 years old and a few years from her planned retirement. She is approaching a critical crossroads and has a lot to think about.

Like Steven and Mario, she isn't an actual client. She's here to help personalize the choices that every government employee has to make when nearing retirement. There is no one universally right answer to the four questions we'll explore below. But the best approach is a thoughtful one that begins years before you actually retire.

Some of the big questions Becky is facing include:

- When should she retire?

- When should she begin to take her Social Security payments?

- How and when should she take withdrawals from her retirement account?

- What should she do with her other government benefits, including her health and life insurance benefits, once she retires?

WHEN TO RETIRE?

When should Becky retire? What factors come into play?

This is the most personal decision of all. Everyone's situation is different. There's so much to consider. For example, how much do you enjoy your job? How financially ready are you to retire? How ready are you mentally or emotionally? A big part of retirement planning is nonfinancial planning. Do you know what you'll do with all that time? Don't neglect that aspect as you monitor your financial preparedness.

Some people can't wait to leave work permanently. It can't happen soon enough for them. However, others form a strong social connection to their workplace that they'll miss. For some of us, our self-identity is closely tied to what we do for work, or perhaps we simply enjoy our job. My observation is that many people doing government jobs—whether they are teachers, nurses, postal workers, or clerks of some kind—are ready mentally and emotionally to enjoy the rest of their life once they qualify for full retirement benefits. Of course, many of them have enjoyed their work and the people they work with, but they're ready to take it easy after 30 or 40 years.

So, here's the big question for many, including Becky: Are they—is she—financially ready to retire?

Let's look at Becky. She began her job in 1992 at age 30 and is covered by the Federal Employees Retirement System.

Although she qualifies for full retirement benefits at age 60 based on her age and having at least 20 years of service, she doesn't feel it's in her best financial interest to retire just yet.

At this point, she thinks she might retire next year, at age 62, once she has the option of claiming her Social Security benefits. However, she doesn't need to commit to that now. She knows that the longer she waits before she starts to collect Social Security benefits, up to age 70, the more Social Security benefits she'll receive each month for the rest of her life.

By committing to keep working until at least age 62, she figures she can make sure that there won't be a gap between earning a full-time salary and replacing that with a combination of her FERS lifetime annuity, her Social Security benefits, and her TSP withdrawals, which is like 403(b) or 457(b) for federal employees. Becky can come back to this decision in a year or two and weigh her options then.

WHEN TO CLAIM SOCIAL SECURITY BENEFITS?

When should Becky begin to take her Social Security benefits? There is a lot to consider here. While she could take them as early as age 62, if she did that, she'd have them reduced by 30 percent for every month for the rest of her life.

Let's assume that Becky could qualify for full benefits of $3,000 per month at her full retirement age of 67 because she earns $125,000 per year. The table below shows how much she'd receive if she were to begin her benefits at ages 62 through 66, based on a reduction of 6.667 percent for each of the first three years, counting down from 67 to 64, and then a reduction of 5 percent for the next two years of claiming early benefits, down to age 62.

If Becky takes Social Security benefits early[7] . . .

CLAIMING AT AGE . . .	FULL BENEFITS OR NET PERCENTAGE OF FULL BENEFITS RECEIVED	MONTHLY BENEFIT	SOCIAL SECURITY BENEFITS MONTHLY REDUCTION
67	100%	$3,000	$0
66	93.33%	$2,800	$200
65	86.67%	$2,600	$400
64	80%	$2,400	$600
63	75%	$2,250	$750
62	70%	$2,100	$900

---

[7] https://www.ssa.gov/oact/quickcalc/earlyretire.html.

And if Becky were willing and able to delay receiving her benefits until age 68, 69, or 70, this is how much more she'd receive in monthly benefits:[8]

CLAIMING AT AGE . . .	FULL BENEFITS OR NET PERCENTAGE OF FULL BENEFITS RECEIVED	MONTHLY BENEFIT	SOCIAL SECURITY BENEFITS MONTHLY REDUCTION
67	100%	$3,000	$0
68	108%	$3,240	$240
69	116%	$3,480	$480
70	124%	$3,720	$720

As you can see, if Becky can afford to wait, and if she believes there's a decent chance that she'll live until at least age 79, it would be in her best interest to wait until age 70 before claiming her benefits. That's what's called the break-even age, which is when the benefit of waiting grows enough to make up for the several years of passing up benefits. Plus, let's say Becky works at her favorite boutique a few days per week because she enjoys the company. If she earns more than $21,240 in 2023, her Social Security benefit would be further reduced by $1 for every $2 she earns above that threshold. That's because age 62 is considered "early retirement" by the Social Security Administration (SSA), and the SSA tries to encourage people

---

[8]   https://www.ssa.gov/oact/quickcalc/early_late.html.

to work until their "full retirement age." For Becky, that's age 67. At that age, she will be able to earn as much as she wants while still collecting her full Social Security benefit.[9]

What Becky would have to do, however, if she decided to retire at age 62 and wait eight years until claiming Social Security benefits is piece together enough income from her FERS life annuity and TSP withdrawals to hold her over until age 70. If that's too many years of sacrificing those benefits, she could consider a number of options, including perhaps not retiring as early as age 62 or not waiting as long as age 70 to start receiving Social Security benefits.

Another option could be to take accelerated or higher TSP withdrawals from age 62 to 70 to buy her time, and then she'd file for the highest benefit so as to increase her monthly Social Security benefits from $2,100 to $3,720 for the rest of her life, beginning at age 70. At that point, she'd receive Social Security benefits and her FERS life annuity, and she wouldn't need to withdraw as much from her TSP.

These are the kinds of questions that are best answered by a certified financial planner, who can illustrate the different options for Becky a year or two before she plans to retire. That way, she can make these one-time-only decisions with confidence.

There is a lot to learn about and consider when it comes to Social Security benefits claiming strategies. Whether you're married, divorced, or widowed is an important factor. Also, certain employers do not provide the opportunity to contribute to Social Security. In fact, according to the National Association

---

[9]   Rebecca Lake, "How to Calculate Your Social Security Break-Even Age," https://smartasset.com/retirement/social-security-break-even-age.

of State Retirement Administrators (NASRA), nearly 25 percent of employees of state or local governments pay into a pension system *in lieu* of Social Security. This is especially common among teachers, firefighters, police officers, and first responders.

NASRA points out, too, that this arrangement is particularly common if you're a public employee in Alaska, Colorado, Louisiana, Maine, Massachusetts, Nevada, or Ohio. In the Washington, DC, metropolitan area, we have federal retirees under the original Civil Service Retirement System who were never allowed to contribute to Social Security. As a result, neither they nor their surviving spouses will receive Social Security benefits.

Later on in the book, we'll illustrate some smart moves people can take regarding Social Security benefits, and in Chapter 8, we'll look at some mistakes to avoid and explain why and how to avoid them. But the biggest mistake may be to assume you're entitled to Social Security benefits only to realize later you haven't paid into them.

Because Social Security benefits are highly important but can require some serious thought and analysis, I recommend taking the time to understand them and make sure you make the best decisions for your situation. This process often starts with obtaining estimates of your pension and Social Security benefits and carefully reviewing them for accuracy. If you spent part of your career in one of these states or positions in which you didn't contribute to Social Security, then once you retire, you could consider working a few more years for another employer in order to contribute to Social Security and improve the benefit you'll eventually receive!

WHAT'S THE BEST WAY TO TAKE MONEY FROM A RETIREMENT ACCOUNT?

Let's move on to the question of withdrawing from a retirement account. There are a handful of ways to turn your accumulated balance into money you can begin to live on. How should Becky transition those assets into income? What are her choices, and what makes the most sense for her and her situation?

Here are four ways Becky could withdraw money from her TSP. They apply similarly if you have a 403(b), 401(a), or 457(b) plan:

1. She could simply leave her money in the plan and let it continue to accumulate, tax-free, until she's forced to withdraw required minimum distributions (RMDs) beginning the year she turns 73. All retirement plans must distribute RMDs unless you're still working and contributing to that plan.

2. She could also take control of her money by moving it to an IRA and continuing to let it grow tax-deferred. By taking a direct rollover in this way, if she does it properly, she can avoid paying any income tax on the rollover. When she needs some money to live on, she will simply request withdrawals from her investment firm, and they'll even withhold taxes. So it's like she's creating her very own paycheck. This option allows her flexibility and control over what's probably her largest investment. She can, of course, work with a financial advisor to help guide her so she can spend more of her time enjoying her retirement.

3. She could convert it to a life annuity. In that case, she would be purchasing an annuity and would receive guaranteed lifetime monthly payments, but she would give up all control of that money and any future growth potential of that money.

4. She could choose to receive payments in regular installments on a monthly, quarterly, or annual basis. Those payments could be based on a fixed dollar amount or based on a life expectancy formula, but the account would continue to grow with the investments.

There's much to think about here. Again, what a great time for Becky or others in her situation to benefit from expert, unbiased advice from a fiduciary financial advisor whom they trust.

WHAT TO DO ABOUT HEALTH INSURANCE AND LIFE INSURANCE ONCE YOU RETIRE?

Becky, like most other government employees, will have access to health insurance that will complement her Medicare B, often called a Medigap plan. Having your employer subsidize the cost of health care in retirement is a huge benefit, often one of the main reasons why people stay in a government job.

In Becky's case, the Federal Employee Health Benefits Program is so robust that some retirees don't even bother getting Medicare B. She also has some life insurance coverage that she will retain in the coming years. She can decide to pay for some extra coverage or just let it dwindle down to 25 percent of her former coverage. We go into more detail about federal retiree benefits in the next chapter, but I have yet to meet a government retiree who didn't appreciate their valuable health and life insurance benefits.

KEY TAKEAWAYS

This chapter has covered a lot. We've taken you through three scenarios that illustrate key decisions you'll make or have made at critical points in your government career—the beginning, middle, and end. Take your time reflecting on these issues. Take the time to learn more.

In brief:

- Learn all you can about your various government benefits.

- Make thoughtful and timely decisions.

- Explore all your choices and the various consequences.

- Do a benefits checkup every now and then to learn about new or different investment or insurance options and to make sure what you're paying for is still necessary.

- If you retire early, be aware of both sides of that coin, and make sure you and your money can go the distance.

- Consider getting objective, professional guidance from a fiduciary financial advisor at any point on your journey.

CHAPTER 5
Benefits from Uncle Sam

Because we're located in the suburbs of Washington, DC, we feel it's important to recognize federal government employees with their very own chapter. Unless you live in this area, you might not realize how your day-to-day life is affected by these hardworking employees. Think about the Food and Drug Administration, NASA, the National Park Service, the National Oceanic and Atmospheric Administration (NOAA), and the Federal Emergency Management Administration.

This alphabet soup of acronyms touches all our lives—often in times of crisis but also benefiting our health and allowing us to explore the beauty of our country and the universe. Federal employees have pension systems and retirement accounts that can be as varied as those of state employees. Typically, a career in the federal government can take you through different departments and agencies. Many people retire from life in the military only to start a new career in another unrelated area such as the State Department. An accountant or attorney might bounce from a government job to the private sector or a nonprofit. The DC area is home to a well-connected network of professionals who are able to apply their skills in so many ways. They might be enticed by nonfinancial benefits, depending on their personal situation.

Now, let's go into a bit more depth and detail. Please note that this is not meant as a comprehensive reference. It's intended as a basic, practical guide that I hope can help readers to better understand and take full advantage of their government employee retirement benefits.

For specific questions about your benefits, it's best to speak with your agency's human resources department or the Office of Personnel Management, or do some of your own research online. The federal government also hosts many seminars and webinars on financial planning, retirement planning, and estate planning, which are led by local financial advisors and attorneys. You could also get further guidance on how to navigate those benefits from a fiduciary financial advisor who is familiar with government benefits programs and with you.

A quick plug here, in case that was too subtle: At Kendall Capital, we serve dozens of clients who are or were employed by federal, state, or local governments. We are here for you if you need us.

There is a lot to consider here. Let's start by reviewing the two major federal government retirement programs: CSRS and FERS.

THE CIVIL SERVICE RETIREMENT SYSTEM

The CSRS is a classic defined benefit pension plan. Available to federal employees hired before January 1, 1984, it provides a guaranteed annuity to government pensioners for the rest of their lives.

CSRS employees are not eligible for Social Security benefits based on their years of federal employment. That's because they didn't have Social Security taxes deducted from their income. They can participate in the Thrift Savings Plan, a tax-advantaged retirement plan like a 401(k) or 403(b). However, unlike employees hired on or after January 1, 1984, who are in the Federal Employee Retirement Savings plan, they don't receive matching TSP contributions.

By now, almost four decades after 1984, just 4 percent of current federal employees fall under the CSRS system, so we won't devote much space to their benefits. However, if you fall into this category, you should know about the Voluntary Contribution Program (VCP).

VOLUNTARY CONTRIBUTION PROGRAM

The CSRS VCP offers a unique opportunity to make large contributions to a Roth IRA. It is available only to CSRS or CSRS Offset employees. FERS federal employees aren't eligible. The program was designed to encourage CSRS employees to boost their savings as they are not eligible for Social Security. It can also provide some flexibility to pay extra bills, which is particularly helpful when you're on a fixed income.

What's truly special about the VCP is that it is a powerful way for CSRS employees to fund a Roth IRA with very few limits, even if they earn too much money to be eligible to normally contribute to a Roth IRA. Eligibility to make Roth IRA contributions for 2023 begins to phase out above a modified adjusted gross income of $138,000 for single filers and $218,000 for married couples who file jointly.

Here's how the VCP works: you are allowed to contribute up to 10 percent of your *accumulated lifetime federal earnings*.

That's not your annual earnings. That's your total accumulated earnings over your career in a federal government job. You can do it through several payments over any period of time or even with a single large check. Because this is after-tax money, there's no tax deduction. The contribution initially goes into a separate VCP account outside of your regular CSRS retirement account.

At retirement, you'll have two choices: either take your savings as a fixed, guaranteed payout though a VCP annuity or transfer it all to a Roth IRA that you can invest yourself. It's an all-or-nothing choice. You can also withdraw or transfer the money at any time before retirement. However, once you do that, you'll no longer be able to open another VCP account.

This is a great opportunity to shift some savings, inheritance, or regular brokerage account investments into the cherished "tax-free" category. It's even better than the Roth conversion strategy you may have heard about because there are no taxes due—as there would be in a conversion from a traditional IRA to a Roth—and the amount you could theoretically contribute is substantial.

This is a little-known retirement option, but if you have cash or investments that could be easily liquidated, then you don't want to miss out on this chance to build a tax-free nest egg to balance out your fully taxable Thrift Savings Plan assets.

EXCEPTIONS: TOO NUMEROUS TO LIST HERE

As noted earlier in the chapter, this book would become long and tedious if we got too far into the weeds of all scenarios regarding the CSRS and/or the FERS. But I want to mention briefly that there are rules covering special cases involving:

- CSRS refunded service,

- Military service,

- Part-time service,

- CSRS offsets (which affect people who had five or more years of service under CSRS and who left and returned after 1984),

- And more.

If any of these exceptions apply to you, it's best to talk with your HR officer or ask a fiduciary investment advisor for guidance.

FEDERAL EMPLOYEES RETIREMENT SYSTEM

The federal government introduced the Federal Employees Retirement System on January 1, 1984. It's similar to the CSRS but has some key differences. Among the biggest differences: the FERS annuity is less generous, but FERS employees pay Social Security taxes and receive Social Security benefits.

Additionally, as noted earlier, the first 5 percent of salary contributions that FERS employees make to the Thrift Savings Plan are matched, amounting to a bonus of up to 5 percent of their salary. By the way, CSRS employees don't receive this match.

Like the CSRS, FERS uses formulas based on the

employee's high-three salary to determine their annuity. Before sharing how that formula works, an important element in retirement eligibility for FERS employees is the minimum retirement age (MRA) calculation.[10]

IF YOU WERE BORN . . .	YOUR MRA IS . . .
Before 1948	55
1948	55 and 2 months
1949	55 and 4 months
1950	55 and 6 months
1951	55 and 8 months
1952	55 and 10 months
1953–1964	56
1965	56 and 2 months
1966	56 and 4 months
1967	56 and 6 months
1968	56 and 9 months
1969	56 and 10 months
1970 and after	57

10   https://www.myfederalretirement.com/fers-mra/.

FERS employees may retire with full benefits at their minimum retirement age with 30 years of service. There are two other eligibility options as well:

1. FERS employees with at least 20 years of service may retire at age 60.

2. FERS employees with at least five years of service may retire at age 62.

SPECIAL PROVISION

As with CSRS, FERS has a special provision for law enforcement officers, firefighters, and air traffic controllers. They become eligible to retire with full benefits at age 50 if they have at least 20 years of special provision service or at any age if they have 25 or more years of service, including at least 20 years of special provisions service. There is also an early retirement provision, called MRA+10.

HOW TO CALCULATE A FERS ANNUITY

Step one: Determine your "high-three average." That's the average annual salary in the 36-month period during which you earned the highest salary. Typically, that would occur during your final three years or 36 months in your job.

Step two: Write down your total years of service.

Step three: Plug those numbers into the appropriate formula below.

There are three formulas:

1. The standard FERS annuity formula

2. An enhanced FERS annuity formula for FERS employees who retire at age 62 or older with at least 20 years of service

3. A FERS special provisions formula for law enforcement officers, firefighters, and air traffic controllers

Standard FERS Annuity Formula:
High three × 1 percent × years of service = annual annuity

Enhanced FERS Annuity Formula:
High three × 1.1 percent × years of service = annual annuity

Special Provisions FERS Annuity Formula:
High three × 1.7 percent × first 20 years of service = A
High three × 1 percent × remaining years of service = B
A + B = special provisions annual annuity

To see how this works, let's look at another hypothetical example: Dan, who retires at age 60 with 30 years of service and a high-three salary of $120,000. Using the **standard FERS annuity formula**, he'd receive an annual annuity of $36,000.

Now, what if Dan waits two more years and qualifies for the **enhanced FERS annuity**? His high-three salary rises to $127,500, and he has 32 years of service. Subsequently, his annuity increases to roughly $45,000 annually. By waiting two years, he'd receive almost $9,000 more per year once he retires. If he lives 30 more years, that could add up to $270,000 more (plus the cost of living allowance, which will be offset by inflation).

Of course, he'd pass up two years of $36,000-a-year standard annuity, so the net increase over three decades would be $270,000 – $72,000 = $198,000. Also, by waiting two years, he'd be able to preserve any savings he has by not having to draw them down during that period. And then there's the potential growth of any investments. Also, he would have two fewer years of retirement to fund. That could allow him to enjoy a more financially relaxed retirement. Perhaps he'd be able to travel more, eat at nicer restaurants, or buy the car of his dreams.

To illustrate how the special provisions annuity works, let's look at Cole, a firefighter who retires with a high-three salary of $75,000 and 30 years of service. His A calculation is $75,000 × 1.7 percent × 20 = $25,500; his B calculation is 75,000 × 1 percent × 10 = $7,500. Therefore, his total **special provisions FERS annuity** is $33,000.

As noted earlier, there are so many exceptions and special situations that we can't cover them all here. So consult with your HR department and/or a knowledgeable fiduciary financial advisor.

MAKE THE MOST OF YOUR CSRS AND FERS BENEFITS

For both CSRS and FERS employees, there are various strategies to try to maximize your annuity. One is to convert any unused sick leave to service days or months. This could result in a larger monthly annuity. For more information, go to the opm.gov website and look for the credit for unused sick leave conversion chart. This is the URL: www.opm.gov/retirement-center/publications-forms/pamphlets/ri83-8.pdf.

Also, if you have any unused annual leave when you retire, the federal government will buy it back, and you'll receive a lump sum based on your hourly rate. This payout could help you with cash flow when you retire as you wait for final adjudication of your annuity, which could take a few months.

If you retire at the end of a calendar year, you could receive the lump sum early in the following year, and if you fall into a lower tax bracket, you could save a bit of money on taxes.

GOVERNMENT BENEFITS AND SOCIAL SECURITY ELIGIBILITY

I have mentioned Social Security benefits only in broad strokes so far. At a very general high level, for federal government employees, Social Security benefits are not available to CSRS employees, but they are an important part of the FERS along with the FERS annuity and the Thrift Savings Plan.

But what if someone spends part of their career in the CSRS or working for some government agency in which employees don't participate in Social Security (no Social Security taxes paid and no Social Security benefits received)? For simplicity, I'll refer to this as a *hybrid Social Security scenario.*

In that case—and this could apply to state pensions as well as the federal system—these retirees could have their Social Security benefits reduced through either the Windfall Elimination Provision (WEP) or the Government Pension Offset (GPO). The WEP reduces Social Security benefits for some retirees, while the GPO can reduce Social Security benefits for spouses, widows, and widowers entitled to them. In either case, the reduction of Social Security benefits is prompted by a hybrid Social Security scenario.

If you have a state or federal pension subject to some offset, you can learn more about the GPO[11] and WEP[12] by visiting the Social Security Administration's website. It's worth noting that some jobs are subject to these provisions while others aren't. For example, in some states, teachers may be subject to the reductions but police officers are not. This may seem arbitrary, but it ultimately has to do with how contracts were negotiated.

BUT WHY?!

Many people think the WEP and GPO are unfair. The reasoning behind them is that without some type of windfall elimination or offset, people in a hybrid scenario would receive overly generous combined benefits, or a windfall, by receiving

---

[11]   Government Pension Offset, Social Security Administration, https://www.ssa .gov/pubs/EN-05-10007.pdf.

[12]   Windfall Elimination Provision, Social Security Administration, https://www .ssa.gov/pubs/EN-05-10045.pdf.

the more generous government annuity that was based on a lack of Social Security benefits plus the Social Security benefits they earned in their other work.

Opponents of the WEP argue that it reduces benefits disproportionately for some households, including those with low income. Others say the current WEP formula is imprecise and unfair and can create a nasty surprise for people who have planned for their full Social Security benefits but who find out in the eleventh hour that those benefits will be reduced.

COULD THE RULES BE CHANGED?

In the past couple of years, a few bills that seek to reform the WEP or GPO have been introduced to Congress. In the near-to midterm, it is possible that the WEP and GPO formulas could be altered, or perhaps they could be eliminated altogether. In the meantime, it's important to check on the status of your benefits and make sure that you have an accurate understanding of what you can expect once you retire.

WHAT IF THERE WAS A MISTAKE? FERCCA MIGHT HELP

What if you made a mistake or there was an administrative error years ago, leading you to enroll in the wrong federal retirement plan? In certain circumstances, you can correct this before, or even after, you retire.

For example, if you change your mind about survivor benefits after you retire, you could actually go back and change that coverage option under the Federal Erroneous Retirement Coverage Corrections Act (FERCCA). FERCCA was introduced a couple of decades ago, primarily to address situations involving choices between the CSRS and FERS systems. But it goes beyond that.

If you qualify through FERCCA, you could potentially:

- Receive reimbursement for certain out-of-pocket expenses paid because of an error in coverage,

- Add makeup contributions to the TSP and receive earnings on those contributions, or

- Be able to benefit from certain rule changes to how your government service is calculated for retirement.

WHAT TO DO ABOUT HEALTH INSURANCE AND LIFE INSURANCE ONCE YOU RETIRE?

There are other benefits that a preretiree must consider as well. Federal employees with at least five years of service can continue their Federal Employee Health Benefits coverage into retirement. They can combine them with Medicare. However, many federal employees with FEHB coverage will find that they're already sufficiently covered without adding Medicare coverage.

Because everyone's situation can be different, it's highly recommended that you do the research and consult with a Medicare specialist to see what's best for you. The FEHB coverage is comprehensive, but there are some supplemental benefits to having Medicare B as well. We recommend considering these options by age 64 so you won't feel rushed or stressed when it's time to decide whether to enroll in Medicare B at age 65. Your human resources department or an independent financial advisor can help answer questions.

As for continued life insurance coverage through the Federal Employee Group Life Insurance program, there are several options once you retire, with a sliding scale of premiums and coverage. You could opt to continue your full basic life insurance coverage for an extra premium. A second option is a 50 percent reduction in coverage for a smaller extra premium. The coverage would be reduced by 1 percent each month from the 100 percent level down to 50 percent roughly four years later. A third option is to gradually scale back coverage by 75 percent, for which you would pay no premium. That option would see your basic coverage reduced by 2 percent each month until it reaches 25 percent of the original full coverage.

I encourage you to take your time and think this through before deciding on the best option for you. It can be helpful to speak with your human resources folks to confirm coverage details and options and receive guidance.

When it comes to the retirement benefits cards that you hold in your hand, it's vital that you know the rules and know how to play the game so that you don't leave any money on the table. But when it comes to federal retirement benefits, you may find yourself in a complicated situation or feel overwhelmed trying to make the right decision. While the federal government tries to educate its retirees and help them with these decisions, the reality is that it's just not that simple.

So if you'd like to consult with someone individually to

help you maximize your federal retirement benefits, consider contacting Tammy Flanagan & Associates at retirefederal.com. She and her colleagues have years of experience working in the federal government and can help advocate for you to correct errors, better understand your options, and avoid common pitfalls.

At Kendall Capital, we don't receive any kickbacks for referrals, but we want this to be a resource for you, especially if you or a family member are in a complicated situation.

MILITARY SERVICE AND VARIOUS BENEFITS OPTIONS

Retirees from a career in the armed forces have a different retirement plan and benefits system. It's not only different from the civilian system. It's also a bit more complicated.

There are actually two retirement systems for those who serve in the US military:

- A legacy "high-36" system for those who joined before January 1, 2006.

- The Blended Retirement System for those who joined the service on or after January 1, 2018.

- Those who joined between those two dates could stay in the legacy system or enroll in the new one.

The high-36 system offers a defined benefit pension equal to 2.5 percent × the number of years of service × the average of your highest 36 months of basic pay. So, if your high 36 was $5,000 a month and you had 20 years of service, you would receive $2,500 a month, or 50 percent of your average monthly pay.

The Blended Retirement System includes a monthly annuity similar to the above but based on a calculation of 2 percent per year served. So using the same example, the retired service member would receive $2,000 a month. In addition, he or she would receive matching Thrift Savings Plan contributions, which could total 5 percent of his or her salary (the maximum match).

That dollar amount would change over the course of a career. But for the sake of a hypothetical example, if you earned an average $40,000 base pay and contributed enough to get the maximum match, that would be $2,000 a year. Multiplied by 20 years and given a chance to compound, that could grow substantially and perhaps even be the rough equivalent of the old system.

This is a classic example of an employer shifting responsibility to employees. We're all being asked or expected to be more responsible for own retirement savings and planning. It seems that we all need to take full advantage of that opportunity. After all, if you don't contribute enough to get the maximum match, you're truly leaving free money on the table. I don't know too many people who want to do that.

Occasionally, we meet clients who served in the military and now work either in the federal government or a private contracting firm. They are essentially starting a whole new career and benefit from both their military pension as well as their current salary. We encourage these clients to maximize their retirement accounts (401(k), TSP, etc.) and build wealth in regular taxable brokerage accounts because that military pension is like having an extra salary.

This is especially important for our younger veterans, many

of whom would benefit from extra care for their physical and mental well-being. Tricare and Medicare cover a lot, but treatments and techniques such as massage, yoga, and flotation therapy work well but are not considered "medically necessary." When you've been through trauma, you might face additional financial pressures because retirement could come sooner than expected, so be prepared.

SEVERAL SPECIAL SITUATIONS

In writing a book like this, it's impossible to cover every situation a government employee might face. The general goal is to provide helpful information and guidance that will apply to a good number of readers. This chapter is an opportunity to address a few special situations with the understanding that they are not exhaustive. The idea is to shed a bit more light on a few circumstances.

The main focus in these examples will be on federal government jobs. If you work in a state or local government job, the details of your situation could be different. Always do your homework and check with your personnel office on rules that govern your situation.

EARLY DEPARTURE FROM A
GOVERNMENT JOB . . . NOW WHAT?

Even if you intend to stay in a government job for your entire career, you might leave that position and move to a non-government job at some point.

There are three options regarding the retirement benefits you will have accrued during your service:

OPTION ONE: RECEIVING A LUMP SUM REFUND

You can take a refund of your FERS or CSRS pension contributions as a lump sum. Just fill out and submit an *Application for Refund of Retirement Deductions* to your personnel office within 30 days of leaving your government job. If beyond 30 days, submit your application to the Office of Personnel Management.

Be aware that you'll pay taxes on that money. Also, taking money that was supposed to pay your expenses in retirement and using it now is strongly discouraged. What if your future self needs that money more than you do now?

OPTION TWO: RECEIVING THAT REFUND PAYMENT AS A ROLLOVER

Another option for that refund payment is to roll it over into an individual retirement account (IRA) or an employer-sponsored retirement plan if you have one at a new job. If you do that, make sure that the rollover is made payable directly to that retirement account. If you're not careful, and the check is payable to you, then you'll wind up having taxes withheld from the withdrawal. If you don't currently have an IRA, you can open one so that you keep this pension distribution tax-deferred.

OPTION THREE: TAKING A DEFERRED ANNUITY

A third choice, available to you if you have at least five years of service and you leave the money in the retirement fund, is to take a deferred annuity after age 62. This is most common because often, employees, especially in the DC area, are recruited to work in the private sector. But, after a while, they may take their new skills and return to the federal government as they often miss the pension and good health insurance benefits.

There are pros and cons to each of the second or third options. Much depends on your situation and your personality as an investor. However, pensions are harder and harder to find these days, and the federal government will be the safest, as the benefit is backed by the strongest financial institution, the US Treasury. Remember, a pension is only as good as the entity promising to pay it.

The key is to make a thoughtful, intentional decision.

PHASED RETIREMENT: A RELATIVELY NEW DEVELOPMENT

In recent years, the idea of phased retirement in a federal government job became a reality for some employees. This can be a classic win-win situation. It allows a full-time employee to work part time, mentoring younger colleagues while starting to receive retirement benefits. Federal agencies, meanwhile, get to retain employees whose institutional knowledge would otherwise be lost.

If you work in phased retirement, you'll have the rare opportunity to draw retirement benefits while earning additional credit for your future benefits. The partial annuity payments you receive are prorated based on the portion of the workweek that you don't work.

While designed as a short-term human resources management tool, phased retirement can also provide new retirees with a softer transition into retirement. It may not be for everyone or every situation, but it can be a great opportunity for some government employees.

WORKING IN RETIREMENT: WHAT IF YOU'RE REHIRED?

Another option for some retirees from a federal government job is to be rehired. In some situations, this could cause your retirement annuity to stop, in which case you'd be treated as a regular employee, and you'd re-enroll for various employee benefits.

If you were covered by CSRS and were reemployed within a year, you'd continue under that plan. If you were in FERS, you'd continue in that current program. In either case, when your reemployment ends, it would be like retiring a second time.

In certain cases, you'd be able to continue your annuity while working, and your pay would be reduced by the amount of your annuity paid for the work period in question. The rules covering this area are complex, so I'll leave it at that, but be aware that this is yet another possibility and another distinctly special situation.

PART 2

CHAPTER 6

Beyond Your Pension: TSPs, 403(b)s, and 457s

Chapter 5 explained the functions of the old and the new federal government defined benefit pension programs, the CSRS and FERS. If you work for a state or municipal government, you likely have a similar type of pension. It would be based on the length of time you work, and you would contribute a percentage of your salary. Pensions offer a fixed payment when you retire and take the worry and guesswork out of investing your money, which can offer a great deal of comfort and peace of mind.

However, living on a fixed income can be a challenge, especially when the cost of everyday items continues to go up. Sure, your pension will likely have a cost of living adjustment (COLA), but that might not be enough. Plus, what do you do when you encounter a sudden extra expense, such as a furnace repair or property tax bill? How do you save for those types of expenses? That's why it's important to go beyond your pension with additional savings.

Depending on the details of your career—including how much you earned, how long you worked for the government, and the type of job you had, along with the respective benefits—that pension will likely not be enough to meet your retirement expenses. The reality is that beginning in the mid-1980s, employers in both the public and private sectors realized they could not continue to promise pensions at a level of 80 percent to 90 percent of one's salary at retirement.

It became clear that employees would have to contribute to their own retirement savings accounts and choose from the many mutual funds and annuity options offered by the investment industry. Like it or not, employees had to learn about these options and make their own investment decisions. At Kendall Capital, we think this is a great way for people to grow their own fortune so they are able to supplement their pension and have the flexibility to withdraw funds for that family vacation or cruise around Australia. They potentially could have far more to spend in retirement than if they relied only on a pension. This chapter can help you understand the supplemental retirement savings options offered by your government employer. It's up to you to decide whether, when, and how to take advantage of them.

Generally speaking, keep the following five points in mind when deciding where to save for your retirement. Remember, you're in the driver's seat now, and the supplemental retirement plans are optional. If you're young and just starting your career, you may prefer to open your own IRA or Roth IRA, giving you the utmost control and easy access to your savings. These accounts allow you to make pretax contributions or after-tax contributions, a decision that will depend in part on your current income and expected income in retirement. They offer additional flexibility and access that the government supplemental retirement plans do not. For that reason, they're often the best place to start saving. By setting up monthly contributions, you can "pay yourself first," with contributions automatically deducted from your checking account.

When evaluating your options, consider these five points:

1. Will my employer match my contribution to the workplace retirement plan? An employer match is like a bonus. Why not take that full bonus?

2. Who are the providers or custodians of the plan? The financial stability or strength and reputation of those financial institutions could affect your confidence level.

3. Are my investment options liquid or easy to change if I leave this job? Flexibility and ease of access are important considerations. You shouldn't face unnecessary restrictions in managing your money.

4. Do I plan to save more than $6,500 or $7,500 per year? If you seek to save more than the annual limit in an IRA or Roth IRA, understand that a 403(b) or 457(b) plan will provide that additional savings opportunity.

5. Should I contribute on a pretax or an after-tax (Roth) basis? A key factor could be your current level of income and stage of your career. Ultimately, you should aim to get the biggest tax break. It's also important to have a balance of tax-free and taxable withdrawals in retirement. That can give you the greatest room to maneuver when considering tax efficiency. These are complex questions that a financial advisor and an accountant can help you answer.

State and local government employees also have defined contribution plans they can contribute to: 401(a) plans, 403(b) plans, or 457(b) plans. Some of these also have an employer matching contribution and may even offer a Roth option. Some people even have access to both a 403(b) plan and a 457(b) plan. That means they are allowed to save up to twice as much as other people, in tax-advantaged savings plans. There are even "special catch-up" contribution options available to some 403(b) participants over age 50, depending on their employer. So, it's all the more important to review your options not just at the beginning of your career but throughout your working years and particularly toward the end, when your income is typically highest.

DOUBLING UP ON YOUR CONTRIBUTIONS IN A 401(K), 403(B), OR 457(B) PLAN

Many government employees have yet another special opportunity to boost their retirement contributions. If you have access to both a 403(b) and 457(b) plan, you are allowed to contribute to both at the same time. That doubles your contribution limit for 2023, for instance, from $22,500 to $45,000. And if you're 50 or older, add another $7,500 for the 403(b) catch-up and $15,000 for the 457(b) catch-up, for a grand total of $67,500.

But wait, there's more! As noted in greater detail later in this chapter under "What You Need to Know about 403(b) and 457(b) Plans," there are also powerful catch-up provisions for each of these plans. For 403(b) plan participants with 15 years of service, you can contribute an additional $3,000 a year for up to five years (or $15,000 in one year if you have not been taking advantage of this "special" catch-up contribution). Similarly, 457(b) plans allow a potential doubling up of contributions in the final three years before retirement age if you hadn't maxed out previous years' contributions.

If you are nearing retirement and in catch-up mode, these are all worth looking into and considering in your savings strategies. It may sound absurd, but if you're a dual-income family, receive a pension from your prior stint in the military, and have fully launched your kids so they're no longer eating you out of house and home, you could benefit from these catch-up provisions and have the cash flow to take advantage of them.

ALMOST EVERYTHING YOU WANTED TO KNOW ABOUT TSPS

Let's start with federal employees and take a closer look at the TSP. The specifics will differ somewhat from those of 403(b) and 457(b) plans, but a lot of the basics are similar. TSPs are also offered to military personnel.

WHAT IS THE TSP?

Created in 1987, the Thrift Savings Plan is an important and easy way to save for retirement as a supplement to the government pension and Social Security retirement benefits. As noted earlier, employees covered by the CSRS are able to save in the TSP, but unlike FERS employees, they don't receive a government matching contribution. For FERS employees, the first 5 percent of their salary that they contribute is matched.

WHY SHOULD YOU SAVE IN THE TSP?

There are several good reasons to contribute to the TSP:

- **To augment your government pension** (and, for FERS employees, Social Security benefits) so that you can maintain your desired lifestyle in retirement.

- **To help protect against the impact of inflation,** which is a wild card. Consider the TSP as an important card for you to play within your retirement savings deck of cards. The unknown variable of high inflation over the coming decades could throw your financial plan out the window as it erodes your purchasing power. The safe approach is to save more rather than less, because you never know. That's the middle-class millionaire approach. If in doubt, save. If you can, save.

  And saving through a TSP, 403(b), or 457(b) is a powerful card for you to play. You hold it in your hand, and by playing it, it can help you to trump inflation and other wild cards, such as unforeseen illness, a pandemic, or forced early retirement.

- **The TSP is very low cost.** The annual expense ratio of TSP funds is 0.04 percent, or roughly one-tenth that of the average retail mutual fund. The difference is an annual cost savings of roughly 0.36 percent per year. On a balance of $200,000, that would be $720 (the difference between an annual expense of $80 in the TSP and $800 on a typical portfolio of mutual funds in an IRA).

Multiply that annual $720 in savings for 30 years, and that's $21,600 even before any compounding or growth in your investments.

- **Convenience.** It doesn't get much more convenient than to be autoenrolled, have automatic salary deferrals made to your retirement account, and to benefit from dollar-cost averaging, which keeps you contributing through autodeferral even when your emotions might otherwise work against that.

- **Employer match.** To receive the maximum government matching contribution in the TSP, you need to defer 5 percent of your annual income. The government automatically contributes 1 percent of your income. Then, on the first 3 percent of your income that you save, you receive a dollar-for-dollar match. On the next 2 percent of salary that you defer, you receive a 50-cent match for every dollar. That adds up to 10 percent of your salary going into your TSP account if you contribute 5 percent of your salary.

    That seems like a wise move to me and a great way to play your retirement benefits cards.

HOW SHOULD YOU INVEST YOUR TSP FUNDS?

The TSP is fairly straightforward in terms of investment choices: there are three diversified stock funds, one diversified bond fund, and one government bond fund; and then there are life cycle funds, which are like target-date funds. They are based on your age and are invested in a mix of the above funds, with the exposure to risk gradually dialed down as you approach retirement.

There is also a new mutual fund window, offering access to more than 5,000 mutual funds, in which TSP participants are allowed to invest up to 25 percent of the value of their TSP account. This option is great for people who want to take a more active role in investing their retirement savings.

When considering investing strategies, the most important factor is your risk tolerance. If you are comfortable with greater volatility, you're better suited to more of your money going to the stock funds. If you are more risk averse, less money in stock funds.

However, also hugely important is how much time you have before you retire, along with how long you expect to live. If you're looking at another three decades before you retire and a life expectancy of another six decades, for example, the vast majority of your investments should be in a diversified mix of stocks because over the long term (10-plus years), they have consistently had higher returns than bonds. A fiduciary investment advisor can help guide you.

See the table on the next page for an overview of your TSP fund options.[13]

---

[13] https://www.myfederalretirement.com/tsp-returns.

LETTER	ASSET CLASS	10-YEAR RETURN AS OF 12/31/22	CONSER-VATIVE MIX (EXAM-PLE)	MODER-ATE MIX (EXAM-PLE)	AGGRES-SIVE MIX (EXAM-PLE)
C	Large-cap US stocks	12.57%	30%	30%	40%
S	Small-cap US stocks	9.72%	10%	20%	25%
I	International stocks	4.95%	10%	10%	15%
F	Diversified bonds	1.29%	30%	30%	15%
G	Government bonds	2.08%	20%	10%	5%
L	Life cycle funds	Variable	Glide path gradually reduces risk	Glide path gradually reduces risk	Glide path gradually reduces risk

The above is intended as a general guideline/example and quick reference, not a recommendation. Everyone's situation is different, and numerous factors should be considered. Also, the most recent 10-year returns may look radically different than the returns in the next 10 years.

TSP BENEFICIARY DESIGNATIONS

Be aware that there are two types of TSP beneficiary accounts: spousal and nonspousal. It's crucial to understand the differences between these beneficiaries and plan wisely.

Spouses who are beneficiaries of a TSP account are able to maintain their beneficiary account for life, essentially treating it as one would an IRA. Their only requirement in terms of distributions is to take required minimum distributions on time.

However, if your beneficiary is not a spouse (i.e., your child), then the options are drastically different. *Nonspouse beneficiaries will have just 90 days to take the proceeds out of a temporary beneficiary account and roll over the balance to an inherited IRA.* If they fail to do this, they will automatically receive the full TSP balance, which will be 100 percent taxable that year. They will miss the opportunity to grow the inherited amount tax-deferred for another 10 years and/or be able to spread the income tax burden over 10 years.

This is a welcome change in policy that the TSP made in 2022. Prior to that, the TSP would force out the nonspouse beneficiary's account as a one-time taxable distribution. We witnessed this in 2019 when a client contacted us to manage his inherited $1 million TSP retirement account. He visited us after his parents had passed away. The father had named his spouse as the beneficiary of his TSP, but she passed away just six months after he did.

Unfortunately, unlike an IRA, back then the TSP had to be disbursed all at once. That son had to receive the full distribution that year and be taxed accordingly.

As a consequence, he reported more than $1 million of TSP

retirement income on top of his current income. As a result, he paid an additional $400,000 of income taxes that year. The sad news is that this was entirely avoidable. Either of his parents could have rolled their TSP retirement accounts into an IRA. Then the son could have taken smaller incremental distributions or let the inherited IRA grow until after he retired but before taking Social Security benefits and RMDs from his retirement accounts.

Now that the policy has been changed to allow for a 90-day "temporary" beneficiary account, beneficiaries who are aware of this option have an opportunity to transfer their account to an inherited IRA with a brokerage firm. However, 90 days isn't very long for a grieving child, sibling, or dear friend to realize they have to make an important decision or face a horrible tax consequence.

Of course, with an inherited IRA, you can take a full distribution as soon as possible as with the TSP, but as you can see, the inherited IRA gives your beneficiaries more options.

ROTH OR TRADITIONAL ACCOUNT?

The next question is whether to receive a tax break when you contribute to the retirement plan or when you withdraw your money. As with IRAs, the traditional TSP offers a tax deduction for contributions, but you'll pay taxes on your withdrawals. With a Roth TSP, it's the opposite: no tax break now (when you contribute), but your withdrawals will be tax-free.

The best general advice is to have a balance—a diverse mix of tax treatment, just as you create diversification in your investments. This is a great topic to discuss with your financial advisor and possibly your tax accountant, as they know the particulars of your situation.

WHAT YOU NEED TO KNOW ABOUT 403(B) AND 457(B) PLANS

So far, our discussion of TSPs has included some specifics that apply only to TSPs and some generalities that also apply to 403(b) and 457(b) plans. Those common features include:

- The need to contribute to these optional savings vehicles to augment your government pension and have flexibility and access to cash when you need it,

- The convenience of payroll deduction salary deferrals,

- The general annual contribution limit of $22,500, and

- Basic catch-up contributions of $7,500 for employees 50 and older, bringing the basic contribution limit to $30,000 for those employees for 2023.

Beyond these basics, there are some major differences between TSPs and these two other savings plans for employees of nonprofits and state and local governments. There are also some notable differences between the 403(b) and 457(b).

Here's an overview of what is unique about these two defined contribution plans. We could subtitle this section, "The Good, the Bad, and the Ugly." Let's start with the good.

THE GOOD

Special catch-up provisions. The 403(b) and 457(b) each offer something extra beyond the usual $7,500 catch-up. Participants in a 403(b) plan who have worked for their employer for at least 15 years may be able to contribute an extra $3,000 a year for up to five years.

The 457(b) plan offers something even more attractive: for the three years leading up to your retirement age, you can contribute up to double the annual contribution limit for each year. However, that extra amount is limited to the difference between your previous actual contribution and the maximum contribution allowed.

For example, if your contribution limit was $20,500, and you contributed $10,000, you now would be able to contribute the basic $22,500 plus another $10,500. In theory, you could contribute up to $45,000 in 2023 if you qualified for this special provision, but only if you hadn't contributed at all in 2022. Also, if you take advantage of this double-limit contribution, you can't also use the regular $7,500 catch-up contribution.

Double contributions. Some government employers offer a 457(b) plan in addition to a 403(b). So, theoretically, these employees could contribute double what a person would normally be able to, or $60,000 for someone over 50 who is able to make the basic catch-up contribution in both a 403(b) and 457(b) plan. I say "theoretically" because not too many people are able to salt away that much money in their retirement savings in a single year. However, if you retired from the military and are receiving your pension after 20 years and go to work for a county police force, for example, you may find yourself in a position to save substantially and make up for lost time.

High total contribution. The 403(b) allows a very generous $66,000 annual limit for total employee/employer contribution. That's $73,500 for employees 50 and older.

Quick vesting. Many 403(b) plans vest money in the account immediately or after a short time period. Some 457 plans also vest contributions immediately. Vesting is a fancy way of saying the money is yours no matter what. If you're unsure of any of your plan's specific rules, refer to the plan documents or ask a human resources officer.

So far, so good. Now the bad . . .

THE BAD

Matching contributions are not the norm. Although some sponsors of 403(b) and 457(b) plans offer employer matching contributions, most don't. And in the case of 457(b) plans, the $22,500 contribution limit includes any possible employer match.

If you determine that you really don't need additional pretax savings, you may prefer to contribute to a Roth IRA and build up savings in a taxable brokerage account instead. As much as we like the power of tax-deferred growth, there are strings attached to these retirement-focused accounts. It may seem like blasphemy, but we often see retirees who have nothing but tax-deferred accounts. In that case, they have to pay income tax on every dollar they wish to spend at income tax rates that might not have dropped much from their working days.

And when they want to pay for that extra vacation or buy a new car, they hesitate because they know the extra cost will require a larger taxable withdrawal than the year before. They become overly concerned with the income tax burden. In contrast, if they had dedicated some of their savings over the years to a regular taxable brokerage account, they would have accumulated another pot of money, which wouldn't be taxed, that they could tap into for those extras.

THE UGLY

Annuities are often offered and should be avoided. If you ask any unbiased fiduciary financial advisor their opinion on annuities, they are most likely to steer you away from them. Why? Variable annuities carry high annual fees (more than 2 percent and possibly much higher), and they can be highly restrictive. For example, if you want to cancel the contract, expect to pay a surrender charge of perhaps 5 percent or 6 percent. In my experience, annuity salespeople often prey on young teachers to get them invested but then do not offer them much service or education. Ironic, isn't it? The local school board decides which 403(b) options to offer, and all too often, they are limited to annuities.

For example, we have a client named Maggie who started saving in a 403(b) account when she first started teaching. She was only given one option, something called a tax-sheltered annuity, and she was wondering why it wasn't performing as well as the overall stock market after 10 years of investing. When we did some research, we explained to her this was an indexed annuity, the kind that limits on the upside as well as the downside.

That may be suitable for a teacher in her 60s edging closer to retirement, but we're talking about a 32-year-old who understood the powerful potential of the US stock market.

The other unfortunate surprise was when we learned that she could not roll over these savings to a different 403(b) option within her school district. Her annuity came with a surrender schedule that applied a penalty on every dollar withdrawn prior to 10 years, even if it was to another retirement account. That's on every dollar. Since she had been contributing with every paycheck, each contribution was made on a different date, so there would never be a time she wouldn't have a penalty.

Why on earth would an employer condone such a product? Is it really appropriate for a 32-year-old with a risk tolerance for stock market volatility? We thought not and searched for an alternative. Fortunately, by this time, the school district did offer additional investment firms. Although she was still limited to an annuity, this one gave the opportunity for more upside potential and had a surrender schedule of only five years.

Annuities are one of two basic investment options in these plans. The other option is mutual funds. So, if you are in a 403(b) or 457(b) plan and have a choice, my general advice is to go with the mutual fund option. It's not bad and certainly not ugly!

Compare the average mutual fund expense ratio within a 403(b) (0.6 percent) with the variety of fees you could pay in a variable annuity, including an annual account fee, a mortality and expense charge, underlying investment fee, an annual fee for a guaranteed income rider . . . maybe these should be called 403-fee plans!

The salesperson who services a 403(b) or 457(b) plan and sells these products is the opposite of a fiduciary financial advisor, who has a legal obligation to put your interests first. The classic annuity salesperson is out to make a commission by selling you a particular product. I'm not saying annuity salespeople are bad. But they aren't necessarily working in your best interest.

I should give a tip of the hat to Montgomery County Public Schools here in Maryland for revamping their 403(b) plan offerings a few years ago. The district did a thorough review of the numerous investment options they had offered over the years and realized they were not doing a good job as fiduciaries for their employees. So they selected Fidelity Investments as their provider because they offered a variety of investment options along with education and customer support. They further took on the monumental task of helping their employees transfer their savings accounts from the numerous investment firms to Fidelity.

This exercise wasn't too bad for the employees who had selected firms that invested in mutual funds. But the ones with annuities had to jump through hoops, obtaining unusual medallion stamps and returning forms within short deadlines. We helped our clients through these hoops, but most employees were trying to navigate on their own, and boy was it frustrating!

But we applaud Montgomery County Public Schools for taking the time to recognize the lack of cohesive support and education around their retirement plans and then choosing a firm that offered fiduciary services and financial planning advice on a variety of levels so they could help both the new teacher at 22 and the seasoned teacher at 62. It would be great if other educational system employers made similar changes on behalf of their hardworking staff.

If you are faced with someone trying to sell you a product like this in your retirement plan, seek transparency by asking straightforward questions, such as:

- What fees will I pay?

- Will I have to pay any penalties if I change my investment choices?

- Do you receive a commission for selling this product to me?

- Do you earn more money selling me one product over another?

Also, review the five points discussed near the beginning of this chapter: Will you receive an employer match? Are you confident in the financial stability of the companies involved in offering the investments? How accessible will your investments be if you leave your job? How much do you think you might contribute annually? And are you more inclined to make a pretax or after-tax contribution?

HOW MUCH CAN AND SHOULD YOU SAVE?

The 2023 limits for all three of these savings options: $22,500 basic contribution plus $7,500 catch-up contributions for those 50 and older. That's a total of $30,000. *That's how much you are allowed to save.*

Keep in mind that some state and local employees are allowed to save in both 403(b) and 457(b) plans. For those younger than age 50, that's an annual contribution limit of $45,000, and for those 50 and older, that's a whopping $60,000 a year.

As for *how much you should save*? A common recommendation is to save 10 percent to 15 percent of your income each year. That's a way to gain a high level of confidence that you are saving enough to be able to retire by your normal retirement age. However, that doesn't take into account situations where you have a defined benefit pension plan. In that case, you might not need to save quite as much.

Another common recommendation—and I endorse it—is to save at least enough to maximize your employer match in a defined contribution plan—401(k), 403(b), 457(b), or TSP. Otherwise, you're walking away from free money.

In summary, if you have the option to contribute to a defined contribution plan—a TSP, 403(b), or 457(b) plan—in addition to your government pension, do so unless you have evaluated your options and decide that at this point in your career, a traditional or Roth IRA will suffice. In general, take every advantage of the additional savings opportunity, the tax-deferred or tax-free savings, and any possible matching contributions. Think beyond your pension!

In so doing, however, make thoughtful decisions about your

investment choices. How you invest and what your anticipated return and expenses are can make an enormous difference in the long run. So dive right in and learn more about investing for the long run. Become familiar with concepts including dollar-cost averaging, market volatility, and compounding growth. Use the tools and resources available from the plan's investment manager, such as Fidelity or Vanguard, and attend webinars if they are offered. Even if you choose to open an IRA, the major investment firms offer a variety of calculators, videos, and newsletters to help guide you. Remember, you're in the driver's seat. The more you learn as you go, the more confident you will be in retirement.

CHAPTER 7
Smart Moves

We all face so many decisions regarding our retirement, first as an employee, then as a preretiree nearing the transition, and again after we have retired. Get to the basics and ask yourself . . . Why should I contribute to my retirement plan? Is it for tax savings or simply the discipline of saving to build wealth? Are there better alternatives? If not, then . . .

- How much should I contribute to my retirement plan?

- How should I invest my money?

- How can I make the most tax-efficient moves?

- How much can I withdraw without raising the risk of running out of money?

To help guide you along your path, here are a dozen smart moves to consider, first as a government employee and eventually as a retiree.

1. Do your homework. Do your research. Find out about your estimated retirement benefits well before your retirement, even a full year ahead. That lead time could help you avoid any nasty last-month surprises regarding your benefits, future retirement income, or eligibility for Social Security. It also allows time to correct any missing months of service, which could take several months to update. *The key here is to use time to your advantage as you make thoughtful benefits decisions.*

2. Ask questions. Ask your human resources department about the details of any financial products that are offered in your plan, particularly 403(b) plans. One thing that matters is whether the financial professional selling these products, particularly annuities, is earning a commission.

Understand the difference between a financial salesperson and a fiduciary. The salesperson generally is motivated to sell more so he or she can earn more of a commission. Where do your needs or interests fit in? In contrast, a fee-based fiduciary has an obligation to put your needs above all else.

The reason for highlighting 403(b) plans is that they often feature products that are more costly than those in plans that are governed by the Department of Labor through a regulatory system known as the Employee Retirement Income Security Act of 1974. ERISA sets standards for most private industry retirement and health plans to provide protection to plan participants. For some odd reason, 401(k)s are covered under ERISA, but 403(b) government plans aren't.

This reminds me of a client we have in Massachusetts, where even the smallest of towns can select their own investment firms to provide 403(b) options. This client had been a teacher in other parts of Massachusetts, so she was used to the idea of opening new accounts when she started a new job. In general, she was able to select the same well-known mutual fund company, which kept things simple for her.

However, with this job in a very small town, she was told there was only one guy who could open 403(b) accounts for their schoolteachers, so she gave him a call and was surprised when he told her she'd have to use an annuity. She couldn't believe that there would be only one investment available to her, so she called me to see if that was even possible.

Unfortunately, it was true. It's up to the employer to select the vendors who offer investments to their employees. There's no law requiring them to offer choices, and there's no law that says the vendor must be a fiduciary. So, if a decision-maker in a small town wanted to play favorites, they could.

But I encouraged her to keep calling around and ask others in the school administration if they knew of alternatives. Sure enough, her persistence paid off. She got the name and number of another provider who could offer mutual funds. It didn't matter that he didn't work for the same firm where she had her other 403(b) accounts. She just wanted to make sure she could roll over her new savings when she changed jobs. This flexibility is often taken for granted in the private sector. She also made sure to tell all of her colleagues that they did, in fact, have options!

Bottom line: be a knowledgeable investor. Go back to the questions in Chapter 6 to decide if you even need to open a 403(b) account. If there's no compelling reason, then build your savings in other types of accounts where you have more control and flexibility.

3. Be an informed consumer. Asking questions is essential, but also make sure that you understand the answers. You should understand any product or strategy that you are invested in—not just annuities but all financial products and strategies. Even if you work with a great financial advisor, don't just rely on that person. Do so from the vantage point of a well-informed financial consumer.

Keep in mind that these options can change over the course of your career, just like they did in our story about the Montgomery County Public Schools system in Chapter 6. If they do, try to roll over your savings or consolidate them into the new options rather than have several smaller accounts.

4. Know the tax implications of your moves. More generally, consider the tax impact of your financial moves and optimize them. Seek out tax-efficient financial strategies to take advantage of during your career and as you enter retirement. Some basics include taking advantage of tax-deferred retirement savings opportunities, such as TSP contributions, especially Roth contributions, with which you benefit from tax deferral and tax-free withdrawals.

Having tax diversification is ideal. This refers to having a decent mix of taxable, tax-deferred, and tax-free assets to choose from in retirement. That way, when you need to take withdrawals from various accounts, you have a variety of options for tax treatment. For example, if your only option is a 403(b) with pretax savings, but you're not in a high tax bracket, then you may be better off adding to a Roth IRA and regular brokerage account or mutual fund instead. Let's say you're a nurse earning $90,000 a year working for a state hospital. Rather than contribute 10 percent of your salary to a 403(b), you could save $500 a month in a Roth IRA and $250 a month in a mutual fund, both via automatic debits from your bank account.

This is a great opportunity to benefit from the insights of an accountant and/or financial advisor. Pardon the pun, but try not to let your financial life get too taxing!

5. Understand and prepare for inflation. Inflation can erode the value of your investments. Understand this and plan your finances with it in mind. There are a couple of key points here. First, when making forecasts or plans regarding your long-term financial needs and the projected growth of your investments, don't forget about the impact of inflation. Over long periods of time, it can seriously eat away at your purchasing power. This is the greatest risk faced by those who plan to rely solely on their pension and Social Security benefits in retirement.

The "fixed income curse" is a double-edged sword. On the one hand, you love the guaranteed monthly income, but on the other, you have no way to pay for unexpected large expenses or the gradual increase in day-to-day costs. Consider big-ticket items such as major dental work every few years or a new roof on your home. If you rely strictly on a fixed income, there will come a time when you'll have to change your habits because your income doesn't cover as much as it used to.

This reminds me of a couple I know living in an upscale neighborhood in northwest Washington, DC. Although it's upscale today, back in the 1960s, when they bought their small home, the neighborhood was very middle class. The husband served his country following World War II, working for 30 years for one of our security agencies. He retired in 1982 on what they felt was a generous pension, and they even had some savings and investments because they lived quite modestly.

But after 30 years of living on his pension, they found themselves scrimping at the grocery store and letting some repairs on the house go a little too long because the pension just couldn't keep up with their rising costs. Hiring electricians and landscapers meant selling some of those investments, and as they were in their 80s and 90s, they were concerned about outliving those investments.

For example, a steady annual 3 percent rate of inflation would cut your purchasing power in half within 24 years. A rate of inflation twice as high—6 percent—would cut your purchasing power in half in just 12 years. Of course, inflation varies from year to year and even from month to month. But in the big picture, keep it in mind so that your planning is realistic. This is also why we encourage our retirees to remain invested in some stocks so they can continue to grow their money even beyond 30 or 40 years of retirement.

Now, how do you manage inflation risk? There are popular products designed to protect against inflation, such as Treasury inflation-protected securities. These bonds pay an interest rate that is pegged to the rate of inflation. Other types of investments tend to rise more in periods of higher inflation. These include commodities, real estate, and precious metals.

Although it's great to have a diversified mix of assets, you don't need to get fancy if you're concerned about the long-term impact of inflation. Just allocate enough of your investments in stocks, which have significantly outpaced the rate of inflation over long periods of time. For example, the long-term average annual return for the S&P 500 Index over the past century or so is roughly 10 percent, while the long-term rate of US consumer price inflation has been about 3.25 percent.

As this book was written, the annual rate of US inflation, as measured by the consumer price index (CPI), was above 7 percent. That's a historically high rate and a sharp contrast to the average inflation rate over the previous decade, during which inflation was below 2 percent. So the long-term trend is important to keep in mind. Yes, you may get a cost of living adjustment with your pension to help keep up with inflation, but it may well be capped at something modest such as 3 percent.

In summary, don't ignore inflation, but don't panic either. The riskiest aspect of inflation is its long-term potential impact on your savings. A diverse mix of investments, including a healthy exposure to stocks, is an effective approach to managing that long-term risk.

For retirees concerned about losing their purchasing power, it can be helpful to monitor your finances and, if necessary, adjust your budget to respond to the impact of inflation. Small, timely tweaks can help to avoid a major makeover later.

6. Prepare a retirement budget. Years before your planned retirement, begin estimating your retirement income and expenses. Those projections will guide you as well as just about anything, and they will become more accurate as you near retirement. I can't stress the importance of this enough.

There are general rules of thumb that say to plan on expenses that are 70 percent or 80 percent, or some other figure, of your preretirement budget. But that advice is too general and vague to be of much help. What's much better is to begin to look at your current budget about five or 10 years before you plan to retire, and then make estimates on what will change once you're retired.

Once you're within five years of retirement, you can get a pretty realistic idea of what your budget should look like. First, tally up your estimated monthly or annual expenses. And then look at your guaranteed sources of income. That would include, for FERS employees, their FERS annuity and their Social Security benefits, for instance. Subtract those guaranteed monthly sources of income from your projected monthly expenses, and the remaining income is what you'll have to provide from withdrawals from your retirement savings and/or other sources, such as some level of continued income.

This budgeting in advance is one of the best ways to establish whether you are financially ready to retire and what your income and expenses—and your lifestyle—will look like.

A good retirement budget isn't a crystal ball, but it could be the next best thing. The picture will become clearer as your retirement gets closer. Without going through the budgeting process, you're just guessing on whether you are financially ready to retire. And a lot of people tend to be wildly optimistic or pessimistic.

7. Optimize Social Security benefits. When should you claim your Social Security benefits? Everyone's situation is different. But it's important to know what you can gain if you delay applying for these benefits. For every year that you claim these benefits before your full retirement age, you'll be penalized. And for every year that you delay taking your Social Security benefits, you'll be rewarded. Remember our discussion about Becky in Chapter 4? The idea is to provide a level amount of income throughout one's retired years, assuming an average life expectancy.

Clients often ask us, "What's the break-even point?" In other words, at what age should they claim Social Security to make the most of the benefits? I reply, "That depends on how many push-ups you can do!" Your current health is the next important consideration, second only to your ability to earn an income.

For people born between 1943 and 1954, the full retirement age is 66; for those born in 1960 or later, it's 67; and for those born between 1955 and 1959, it's staggered between 66 and 67. If you were to wait until 67 to claim your retirement benefits, you'd have to reach about age 79 to "break even." In other words, after age 79, you'll be glad you waited until your full retirement age to claim your benefits, rather than taking them at 62.

As a couple, in most cases, it's best to have the partner or spouse who has earned the highest benefit wait until they turn 70 to claim benefits. That will also ensure that the other spouse receives the highest benefit possible if the spouse with the higher benefits passes away. Remember, when you both collect Social Security benefits, when one passes away, the surviving spouse keeps only the higher of the two benefits.

8. Can you delay your gratification? Of course, not everyone can wait, and frankly, most people don't want to wait. Delayed gratification seems contrary to our most basic desires. Whatever it is that we want, we generally want it now. Whether it's a pint of Ben & Jerry's ice cream or our Social Security benefits.

Roughly one-third of us sign up for Social Security at age 62. These millions of people are either willingly or unwittingly accepting a 30 percent reduction of their benefits every year for the rest of their lives.

For example, we have a client who was financially ready to retire at 60. He was a great saver, he had no wife or kids, and he lived within his budget. When he turned 62, he really wanted to claim his Social Security, and we showed him the analysis of why it makes sense to wait, especially since his father was still alive at 92. But because he had just lost a dear friend to a heart attack, he felt it was important to start to reap the benefits he had paid into for 40 years. He appreciated our efforts to show him his options, but he was still willing to give up the higher payout in the event that he lives as long as his dad.

9. Maybe you have a good reason to claim benefits early.

There are a couple of valid reasons for claiming Social Security early: you might really need the money or you are in ill health and strongly doubt you'll make it to age 80, which is roughly the break-even age, after which you'd be ahead financially by having waited for your benefits.

Other than that, think about what is best in the long term. Just because you retire at or before age 62 doesn't mean you need Social Security benefits to get by for a few years. Look at your entire financial picture, and consider how you might bridge that income gap. One option would be withdrawing from your retirement savings. Or you might take a part-time job for a few years to get you through that period. There are many possibilities.

What if your spouse passes away? An important note is to

understand that we're discussing *retirement benefits* here. Social Security also provides *survivor benefits*, which have their own rules and amounts depending on your ages and whether there are dependent children. It's a smart move to learn the difference should you unfortunately lose your spouse before either or both of you reach your full retirement age. Without getting into the weeds, I'll highlight here that you are allowed to claim a survivor benefit and then switch to your own retirement benefit at age 70. That will help you maximize your Social Security benefits overall. However, there are penalties for claiming survivor benefits at an early age, too.

My main point here is for you to thoughtfully consider all your options instead of going for an immediate fix of that alluring Social Security chocolate fudge ice cream. Working through various scenarios with a fiduciary financial advisor could lead to an even more satisfying result in the long term.

10. Consider working for a year or two longer. Just one or two years of additional income and savings—and less time withdrawing from your life savings—could make a big difference. You might feel like you are done working! I get it. But if you still enjoy working, even if it means changing careers, an extra year or two in the workforce and reduced time in retirement might shift the financial balance tangibly. Not only would you have less fear of outliving your money; you also might be able to live a bit more lavishly.

For example, let's assume you live to age 90. Instead of retiring at age 63 with $800,000 in your nest egg and needing that money to last 27 years, you decide to work for two more years. During those two years, you continue to contribute to your retirement account while allowing the balance to grow.

At the same time, your government annuity continues to grow, along with your Social Security contributions. Perhaps the net effect of all that is another $100,000 or $150,000 in combined retirement savings and annuity/Social Security benefits. Meanwhile, you would have two fewer years in retirement to fund.

All of that might add another $6,000 to $8,000 or more in total annual retirement income. This could put an extra shine on your golden years. This delayed gratification might not be for everyone, but it could be a difference maker.

11. Maximize spousal benefits. It is important to coordinate a benefits strategy with your spouse or partner whenever possible. You can do this by taking into account both your benefits and those of your spouse or partner and seek ways to optimize the two as a couple.

When it comes to your government benefits, if one spouse has access to a pension and the other doesn't because they work for a company with a 401(k), then it makes sense to take greater risk in the 401(k). That allows for potentially higher earnings and provides a complementary balance to the reliability of the pension's future payout. As a couple, thinking about your investments holistically is important and can be beneficial.

12. If in doubt, save more. There are many unknowns in the field of financial planning and retirement planning. We don't know what the rate of inflation will be in years to come. We can only guess or estimate what the impact of taxation will be because tax rates and tax brackets can change. It can be difficult or impossible to predict a sudden job loss or foresee a major illness that could lead to burdensome medical expenses, such as long-term care.

There is one universal answer: if in doubt, save more. You never know when you'll need the money or what for. I have met few people who have complained to me that they should have saved less money for their future.

I'll end this chapter with an upbeat client story that shows the value of saving aggressively at a young age.

THEY MADE THE MOST OF THEIR SAVINGS PLANS

Jack and Emily are a couple in their early 30s. They both recently completed their respective residencies after medical school. They were used to a modest lifestyle because for the past six years, they were either paying for or borrowing for medical school. Then, during their residencies, they earned very modest salaries.

Shortly after they finished their residencies, in early 2018, they bought a house. When COVID-19 hit, they were working at the hospital as general care doctors. They worked long and hard hours, and they were well compensated; each earned over $200,000 per year.

Jack's grandfather passed away in 2018, and they received a large enough inheritance in a taxable account that they felt—and we agreed—that they could aggressively contribute to both their respective 403(b) and 457 retirement accounts. In a few short years, with each of them contributing the maximum to their 403(b) and 457 accounts, they had combined retirement savings of more than $700,000. Not a bad place to be for a young couple still shy of their 35th birthdays.

Putting this money away so aggressively while they are so young will give them many more options in the future. For example, they could potentially cut back on their hours while raising a family, and they will enjoy the long-term benefit of having a large chunk of money grow tax-deferred for many years to come.

CHAPTER 8
Common Mistakes to Avoid

Y ou've heard the expression, "It's human to make mistakes." While that's true, it is possible to avoid mistakes or at least to be aware of common mistakes and try to avoid them. That's what this chapter is about.

Here are 12 common mistakes in retirement planning for government employees. In some cases, a lack of timely action could hurt your financial future. In other situations, not paying enough attention could lead to subpar or even terrible results. Be aware of these common mistakes, and try to avoid them.

1. Waiting too long to begin to save. Beware of the hefty cost of waiting to act. The sooner you sign up and begin saving in a defined contribution plan, such as the Thrift Savings Plan, the better. But are you aware of how much better?

I'm using a hypothetical example here based on modest retirement plan contributions of $200 a month and a long-term 8 percent return on investment. Jim and Ralph are colleagues. They are both 40 years from retirement. Jim starts saving $200 a month in his retirement plan, earning 8 percent a year. Ralph waits five years before saving $200 a month, so the total amount he initially contributes to his retirement account is just $12,000 less than Jim. This is based on not making a total of $2,400 in yearly contributions to his savings plan. Because he misses out on those first five years of compound returns, that gap will keep growing and growing over the next 40 years.

Any guesses on what their respective total nest eggs will be based on the above assumptions?

Ralph's 35 years of compounding on his $2,400-a-year contributions results in a balance of $431,270. Not bad at all. However, that's $217,000 less than Jim's grand total of $648,360.[14]

By waiting just five years to begin saving for his future, Ralph will miss out on roughly $217,000 in compound growth. And that difference likely will continue to grow through retirement.

2. Investing too conservatively. Next to not saving at all or waiting too long before you begin, another very costly mistake is investing too conservatively for a long-term goal. I appreciate that some people are conservative investors by nature. But the so-called "safe" low-yielding investment can actually be much riskier over the course of your lifetime.

Don't confuse volatility (up-and-down, generally short-term market movements) with such critical concerns as longevity risk (the chance you'll outlive your money) or inflation risk (the danger of your purchasing power being eroded).

Let's look at two more people in this hypothetical example. First, let's revisit the rule of 72, which I mentioned earlier in

---

[14] Time vs. Savings Calculator, Corebridge Financial, https://www.corebridgefinancial.com/rs/home/financial-education/education-center/tools-and-calculators/cost-of-waiting-to-begin-savings-calculator.

the book and which lets you quickly see how long it would take your money to grow at various rates of return. Just divide the number 72 by your annual interest rate. If you earn 4 percent, your money will double in 18 years. And if you earn 8 percent, your money will double in nine years.

I'll keep this simple. Maria and Suzanne each have $10,000 and will invest it for 36 years. Maria invests her $10,000 at a steady return of 4 percent. It doubles to $20,000 in 18 years and doubles again in another 18 years, growing to $40,000. Suzanne, in contrast, invests more aggressively and earns 8 percent a year. In nine years, she has $20,000. In 18 years, her money doubles again to $40,000. At 27 years, she has $80,000. And after 36 years, Suzanne's initial $10,000 has grown to $160,000.

Here we have two people with the same initial investment of $10,000. The seemingly safer investment—perhaps bonds—grows to $40,000 in 36 years. And the so-called riskier investment—stocks—earns twice as much, growing to $160,000, four times greater because of the power of compounding as illustrated in the rule of 72.

Conservative investments are ideal for short-term goals, for which you can't afford to lose what you've been working hard to save. But for the long term, being overly cautious could mean missing out on opportunities for long-term capital growth in the stock market. If you don't expect to begin to spend your retirement savings for a few decades, for example, some short-term volatility will most likely not be much of a factor many years later because your investments will have plenty of time to recover from losses. If you really need to be conservative with long-term investments, then understand that you'll likely need to save more money along the way to reach the same monetary goal.

3. Confusing maximum match and maximum savings. A common piece of advice is to contribute enough to your retirement plan to get the full employer match. While that's good advice, why stop there? If you're able to contribute more, you'll have a more financially sound retirement.

Let's assume you earn $60,000 a year and contribute just 1 percent more of your salary beyond the basic 5 percent you would need to contribute to receive the full government match. Over the course of 30 years, based on a hypothetical 8 percent rate of return, that $600 a year (1 percent of $60,000) would grow to $75,000. Contribute 2 percent more, or $1,200 a year, and that would compound to $150,000 over 30 years. Then, based on a 4 percent annual withdrawal rate, that $150,000 could produce $6,000 in annual retirement income over the following 30 years or so.

Although you wouldn't receive any more "free" money in terms of a match, you would certainly benefit from a larger nest egg.

4. Having a false sense of security. Some employees in a government defined contribution pension might assume that because the government is a financially secure entity, all of the underlying investments in a savings plan are secure. That is not always the case.

It's not the employer's stability that determines the strength of an investment. For example, if you invest in an annuity with high expenses, that might lead to a low net return. Or what if you invest in a volatile fund that suffers investment losses? It might be a concentrated equity fund that is poorly managed or just has a few years of subpar performance. The fact that it's offered through a government-sponsored retirement plan isn't relevant. What matters is the quality of the investments themselves.

For instance, within the context of the historically difficult investment environment in 2022, for both stocks and bonds, we all received an important reminder that even though we might expect a certain level of returns, that doesn't always happen. Markets will rise, and markets will fall. How we respond to volatility and uncertainty will make the greatest difference.

The lesson here is not to assume too much. Always do your due diligence. I don't know much Latin, but I know this expression: *caveat emptor.* Let the buyer beware. In this case, you, the government employee, have to be a smart consumer. Don't rely on anyone else.

About #5 and #6: *The next two points might seem contradictory, but the ultimate takeaway is to find a middle ground between trying to do too much on your own and relying too heavily on someone else.*

5. Being too much of a do-it-yourselfer. Although I will admit up front that I have a bias in promoting the use of a financial advisor, I feel similarly when it comes to remodeling a home, repairing a vehicle, or representing yourself in a contentious divorce.

There are times when the money you might save by doing things yourself could lead to really bad or costly results. In investing, the price of poor decisions or missed opportunities is known as opportunity cost. It might be difficult to quantify them, but they can be enormous.

In remodeling a home or doing car repairs, you might

actually do such a bad job that you need to hire a pro afterward to correct your mistakes. Even worse, a mistake you make in replacing your brake pads could lead to a motor accident. Improper wiring in your home could lead to a house fire. Representing yourself in a contentious legal battle against a sharp lawyer might be emotionally draining, costly, and ill-advised.

Know your limits. In each case, the fees that you pay a professional could lead to a better result in the long run and be well worth the cost.

6. Relying too heavily on others. On the other hand, being an informed consumer will help in many of these cases. If you rely too heavily on a mechanic who might be unscrupulous, or a home remodeling contractor, or a divorce lawyer, or an investment advisor, you might end up with something you're not satisfied with.

Maybe you can use a less expensive aftermarket auto part. If an issue comes up when redoing your kitchen or bathroom, you obviously should have input. After all, you'll have to live with the final result. Similarly, in a divorce, an earnest lawyer representing you might want to win at all costs, while you might see value in compromising rather than attempting to win every battle.

Similarly, in an investment plan, you absolutely should bring your own preferences to the table. A good financial advisor should listen to you and then help by applying his or her skills while taking into account your preferences and needs. To be a good client, you should be informed and not overly reliant on your advisor while being open to their advice.

Also, pertaining to couples, it's important for both partners in a marriage to be knowledgeable about and have input on their finances. Relying too much on your partner to make all the financial decisions could lead to a situation where you are vulnerable and ill prepared in the event of a divorce or the death of your spouse.

7. Failing to plan fully for retirement. As you enter retirement, you're about to go through the biggest change in your life. Make sure you think it through. There are a number of areas where people can make significant mistakes.

Do you know if you have enough money to live on? The best way is to prepare a retirement budget as noted in the previous chapter. Review that basic financial planning exercise and put it into play. You can then determine whether your retirement savings and various benefits are sufficient. If not, think about how you can shore up your finances. One option is to keep working a bit longer. Other possibilities include planning to work part time in retirement or trimming your costs.

Beyond that, there are a lot of little details to think about. Where and how will you live? Money could influence this decision, as well as family, friends, and your lifestyle. What are your priorities? Living close to family? Living in a less expensive city? Being somewhere warm? Having enough money to get away for the winter every year?

After working for your entire career, how will you transition into a world of either leisure or different priorities and interests? Make sure you're ready.

8. Not planning cohesively or as a couple. Financial and retirement planning take a fair amount of thought and planning.

Plans don't come together instantly, or in a single session, or even in two or three. It's an ongoing process. Done well, your retirement plans should be thorough and fairly comprehensive.

A mistake some people make is to consider their own situation but not incorporate their spouse or partner. If you work for the government, for example, and your spouse works in the private industry, how can you combine or coordinate your benefits to get the most out of them as a couple?

Be aware of Social Security rules that could mean that you'll be better off taking spousal Social Security benefits (50 percent of your spouse's benefits) rather than your own benefits. Understand that if you do this, you will gain no additional benefit if you delay claiming Social Security spousal benefits beyond your full retirement age. The maximum spousal benefit is half of your spouse's benefit at full retirement age. If you claim a spousal benefit earlier (between age 62 and your full retirement age), the normal reductions to Social Security benefits will apply.

Another possible mistake in this area is not realizing that divorced seniors who are 62 years and older can receive benefits based on their ex-spouse's record, but only if they remain unmarried. This takes no benefits away from your ex-spouse. It is your optional benefit if it applies. So be aware and look into this if it could apply to you. Also, understand the advantage of waiting until your full retirement age to claim your benefits or even delaying them until age 70. The longer you wait, the more you'll be rewarded, with higher and higher monthly benefits based on your career earnings and Social Security contributions.

The importance of making the smartest decision possible regarding your Social Security benefits is one of the best reasons to consider hiring a professional financial advisor. The decision on when to claim these benefits can be complicated and is irrevocable. At Kendall Capital, we use specialized software as part of the financial planning process. In addition to our expertise and knowledge, our clients benefit from this powerful analytical tool. We want them to be able to make the best decision for their individual situation.

9. Unwittingly not electing a joint annuity recipient for your pension. You might have a reason for not opting for joint annuity survivor benefits on your government pension, choosing instead a single-life benefit. But in some cases, this could be a very costly oversight.

As a government employee with a defined benefit pension, you can opt for *a single-life benefit, a joint and survivor benefit, or a couple of other variations*. With a single-life benefit, monthly payments stop when you die. With a joint and survivor benefit, monthly payments continue through your lifetime as well as your spouse's. The one advantage to choosing the single-life benefit is that the monthly benefits are higher. But leaving a surviving spouse with no ongoing benefit is a terribly high price to pay.

There are other options that modify these benefits. For example, a joint and 50 percent survivor "pop-up" annuity provides an additional benefit. If your beneficiary dies before you, your benefit pops up to the higher amount that you would receive in a single-life annuity.

A certain-and-continuous annuity is another variation that, in the event that you die within a certain period, such as five, 10, or 15 years after your benefits begin, allows your designated beneficiary to receive a benefit for the remainder of that period. However, if you die after this period, there is no survivor benefit.

This is such a big deal that federal plans are required to pay a spousal benefit unless they receive a signed consent form or waiver stating that the spouse chooses not to receive survivor's benefits.[15] Note that state and local government pensions are not covered by this provision, which is why I am flagging it here.

10. Expecting to receive your pension immediately. Don't expect to receive your first pension check right when you retire. It could take half a year or even longer for the federal Office of Personnel Management to process this. I understand that any delays with state and local pension benefits tend to be minor, taking no more than a few weeks.

So plan on covering your expenses with other sources of income during those first few months of retirement, particularly after you officially retire from a federal government job.

11. Overlooking your retirement health care needs and costs. Health care costs can be substantial in retirement. Make sure you know your benefits, and be ready to supplement them if that makes sense.

Federal employees who have five years of service immediately before retirement can keep their health insurance benefits through the Federal Employee Health Benefits Program. You'll have a choice regarding enrolling in Medicare Part A and B, with the option to be covered under FEHB or Medicare.

---

[15] Pension and Survivor Benefits, Women's Institute for a Secure Retirement, https://wiserwomen.org/resources/retirement-planning-resources/pension -and-survivor-benefits/.

Check on your government health insurance coverage if you're a state or local government employee. Because Medicare coverage is complicated and involves numerous options, the best general advice is to explore all your options and make a thoughtful decision on what is best for your situation.

12. Not planning for the impact of taxes. It's impossible to predict what changes might occur to tax rates in the future, but at least be aware of the possibility that income tax rates could rise.

Based on fluctuations to your annual income, however, even with no changes to tax rates, you might see your taxes rise or fall as a reflection of changes to your income. Although most retirees expect their tax bracket to be lower once they retire, that isn't always the case.

For example, you might continue to work, even part time, while drawing a pension annuity benefit and taking Social Security benefits and/or having to take required minimum distributions from a traditional (non-Roth) individual retirement account or defined contribution 401(k) or 403(b) plan. In some cases, income from all of those sources could add up to more than you earned while working full time.

Depending on your age when you take Social Security benefits, you might lose some of those benefits. But at any age, your Social Security benefits are largely taxable. For example, up to 85 percent of Social Security benefits are taxable for individuals with gross income of $34,000 or more or couples filing jointly with gross income of more than $44,000.

Also note that taxation of military pensions varies state by state. So check on your state's taxation policies if this might apply to you.

As I have noted earlier, it can be wise to have a mix of retirement assets based on their tax treatment. That includes accounts that have taxable withdrawals and others with tax-free withdrawals. Depending on your tax situation in any given year, you'll be able to make a strategic decision as to whether taxable or tax-free withdrawals make more sense for you.

Here's a client story that illustrates the consequences of not having that tax diversification or flexibility:

DON'T PUT TOO MUCH INTO RETIREMENT ACCOUNTS

We have a client couple who both worked for a state university in Maryland. Don was a full-time professor at the university, and Brenda worked as an office manager within the university. Don earned about $125,000 annually, and Brenda earned roughly $85,000. As a full-time professor, Don could expect to receive a pension of $58,500 or so. Although Brenda would not have a pension, they would each receive about $32,000 annually in Social Security benefits at full retirement age. At retirement, their combined retirement income of his pension and their total Social Security benefits was expected to be $122,500 before taxes and the cost of health care. The pension and Social Security benefits would be adjusted for inflation.

Because they worked for the state, Don and Brenda were able to put money aside in a 403(b) and 457 pretax savings account. By their early 60s, they had saved more than $1.5 million in these various retirement accounts. That is great because a modest distribution from their respective retirements would allow them to maintain their preretirement lifestyle.

However, they had no other savings outside of these accounts. We recommended that they stop their aggressive retirement saving so they could build up after-tax savings. That would give them more cash-management flexibility during retirement. For example, they could delay taking their Social Security benefits while executing various Roth conversion strategies after retiring and before required minimum distributions from their retirement accounts.

Before they retired, these two state employees sold their home to take advantage of the major jump in home prices during 2021. However, because they had very little home equity and no after-tax savings, they were not able to buy a new home and had to rent during their last few working years.

The lesson here is that too much of a good thing can sometimes be a bad thing. It is best to have a holistic or comprehensive view of your personal finances, which is something that a trusted, objective financial advisor can help with.

CONSULT WITH A TAX SPECIALIST

These are all general pieces of advice or guidance. When it comes to specific tax-related questions, it's always good to consult with a tax specialist.

CHAPTER 9

Some Things to Think About before You Retire

There is much to think about before you retire. As the expression goes, the devil (or God) is in the details. In other words, pay attention to the small stuff before you retire because it could make a big difference. This chapter takes you through several critically important questions that preretiree government middle-class millionaires should consider in the months and years before they retire.

Are you **financially** *ready to retire?* It's a simple question, but it may not be that easy to answer. So many variables come into play. Are you financially secure? Will you be able to replace your salary with enough income to meet your expenses in retirement? Are you psychologically ready for the major changes ahead of you?

The old framework of working until you reach age 65 went out the window years ago. One size truly does not fit all when it comes to the decision of when to retire.

Government employees have additional options that can allow them to receive their full or "unreduced" retirement benefits by age 62 or 60, or even earlier in some cases. Certain government positions provide for full benefits at an earlier age in recognition of both the physical toll that those jobs can take and to reward these workers. This pertains to police officers, firefighters, and some other jobs.

When can you retire with full benefits? This is not an easy question to answer as it will vary based on a variety of factors such as employer, job type, and when you were hired. However, typically, there's a formula based on the number of years you worked in a government job and your age. For example, a federal employee would be eligible for their pension given these scenarios:

AGE	YEARS OF SERVICE
Under 60	30+
60	20
62	5

However, many state and local governments will have a sliding scale that allows you to retire with reduced benefits based on fewer years of employment. For example, our local school system offers larger health insurance subsidies the longer one works. You would want to know if working just one more year, for example, might lead to significantly lower health insurance costs.

Are you emotionally **prepared to retire?** Some people are psychologically ready to retire, but they are not financially ready. For others, it's the opposite. They have the money to retire, but they might not be ready mentally or emotionally. Here's a simple but critically important question: *What will you do all day once you're not working?*

For some people, the list of things they'd like to do is long. You may have a calling that you've put on the back burner. Perhaps starting a business or volunteering with skills you've developed during your career. You might look forward to learning something new, such as playing an instrument or learning how to speak Italian before you take your dream vacation to Tuscany. You will have more time for your passions, such as gardening, writing, painting, or performing in community theater. Maybe you place a high priority on spending time with grandchildren and other family members and friends. Hopefully, you'll stay physically active and play more golf, tennis, or pickleball.

Some people retire and are simply relieved not to have to go to work anymore. But then what? Some retirees sit and watch soap operas or are glued to the cable news. If that works for you, great, but I have met a few people who, after doing that awhile, felt that they needed more of a purpose, something to make them want to get out of bed in the morning.

Winston Churchill once said, "You make a living by what you earn; you make a life by what you give." We often speak to our clients about their goals and interests and share what we've learned from the retired clients who have come before them.

I recently read a comment on an article about phased retirement. I was floored by what I read. The commenter wrote,

"Retirement is just a waiting room for the morgue." This person just wanted to keep working until his dying day. He saw no point in not working.

Heaven help me! If that's all there is to life—work followed by death—well, that's a very sad state of affairs. So, spend some time before you retire making sure that you don't just spend your remaining years in a waiting room for the morgue.

The nature of this book is largely financial planning. That's my area of expertise. However, a book on retirement planning would be incomplete without paying some attention to nonfinancial planning aspects, including taking care of one's health and maintaining social connections.

Could early retirement simply mean a career change? Just because your career in a government job is over doesn't mean your working days are done. As noted above, some people choose to pursue another line of work after leaving their government job. They might need the money or additional benefits, or they might just have a desire to keep working but in something new.

That might mean using your skills in a different setting, such as the retired police officer who then went to work for an intelligence service. Another possibility is to hone your skills or learn new ones. Imagine the stimulation and challenge of pursuing something entirely different. That might even mean becoming an entrepreneur. Is there an entrepreneur inside of you just waiting for a chance to create and build a new business?

What a great time to reflect on where your passions and skills might lead you.

QUICK CHECK-IN ON EARLY RETIREMENT

1. Understand all of your options regarding early retirement. Just because you are eligible for full benefits doesn't mean you have to take them at your earliest opportunity.

2. Know the rules that govern your situation and your benefits as well as all your options.

3. Keep in mind that if you are nearing retirement, you should go beyond your financial plan and also have a life plan. How will you spend your time as well as your money after you leave work?

SOME MORE THINGS TO THINK ABOUT

Here's a review of some critical details that government employees should make sure they have taken care of before they retire.

Make sure you know what your retirement benefits will be.
There's an old saying that when you assume something, you make an "ass" out of "u" and "me." It's a colorful—and memorable—way to remember not to assume too much.

That applies particularly to something as critically important as your retirement benefits. Don't assume anything. Confirm when you will be eligible to retire. Decide when you want to retire. And then, importantly, verify what your actual benefits will be. How much will you receive in your retirement annuity? How much will you have in your TSP, 403(b), or 457(b) plan? And how will you take those assets?

There are a number of key decisions to make and details to review. First, be sure that you know exactly what your retirement benefits will be. Make sure there are no mistakes or oversights in your personnel file. Speak with your human resources department and review your files to verify that all your records are complete, accurate, and up to date. All of your service hours should be checked along with your insurance coverage. There might be seminars offered by your employer on topics such as the retirement annuity (pension) and health insurance benefits for retirees. Make sure you attend them well before you reach retirement age.

COLAs are sweet, but they're not all the same. When doing retirement planning and budgeting, consider the impact of inflation on both your expenses and income sources. On the one hand, it's important to account for the impact of inflation on your future purchasing power. On the other side of the ledger, certain cost of living adjustments are made in order to help retirees keep up with rising costs.

Specifically, both Social Security benefits and the original federal annuity under CSRS have a COLA that is pegged precisely to the annual rate of inflation as measured by the official consumer price index, which is updated monthly by the US Bureau of Labor Statistics.

However, the FERS annuity has a more complex calculation that is based on the COLA but doesn't capture it 100 percent:

- In years when the CPI rises less than 2 percent, the FERS COLA equals the annual CPI.

- In years when the CPI increase is between 2 percent and 3 percent, the FERS COLA is 2 percent.

- In years when the CPI is greater than 3 percent, the FERS COLA is 1 percent less than the CPI increase. For example, the FERS COLA for 2022 was 4.9 percent, while the CPI for 2021 was 5.9 percent. Accordingly, both Social Security benefits and the CSRS annuity rose 5.9 percent for 2022.

Many state and local pensions include a COLA as well, but it could be capped at 3 percent in a given year, for example. So, check the fine print on your pension benefits, and don't assume it's the same for you as it is for a colleague who has been working longer. As we've said before, government employers tend to renegotiate benefits for their employees over the years, and COLAs may have been reduced to save money.

How will you manage your retirement assets? Before you retire, you'll need to decide what you'll do with your employer retirement accounts. In many cases, you can choose to leave them and continue to manage your investments as you always have. Decide whether you should withdraw some money now or wait until you're forced to take your required minimum distribution. Either way, remember to periodically check that your beneficiaries are correct, especially if your plan provider changes.

If you would like to have more investment options and develop a personal relationship with a financial planner, you'll be allowed to roll over your retirement account to an individual retirement account. Doing a rollover is a nontaxable event as you're not withdrawing money to spend but merely changing the firm that holds the account.

As we've discussed, not only will the financial planner be able to provide you with a personalized income and investment strategy, but having an IRA can give you more flexibility to take advantage of wealth management strategies.

For example, a Roth conversion involves converting some savings from a traditional (pretax) IRA to a Roth IRA. You'll pay some taxes today in order to have tax-free income later on. IRAs also allow you to make tax-free donations to charities rather than pay taxes on distributions. These are called qualified charitable distributions, and if you're charitably inclined and over 70.5 years old, you are eligible to make these QCDs in lieu of RMDs. Your TSP, 403(b), or 457(b) accounts do not have as much flexibility as IRAs. Don't you just love our alphabet soup of terminology?

Naturally, you may want to start to receive some money to live on right away. Here's where I suggest you take a step back and look at all of your investment accounts. Be aware that your withdrawals will be taxed if you made pretax contributions to your retirement savings account. However, Roth account withdrawals will be tax-free. Knowing that, every dollar you withdraw from a pretax account will help you estimate your income tax liability. With proper planning, you can have an accurate amount of federal and state taxes withheld from each payout.

Evaluating how to take your retirement savings plan assets is the kind of decision that could be made easier with the help of a trusted financial advisor. We'll discuss the benefits of working with one a bit later in this chapter. However, we encourage you to simplify and consolidate whenever possible. After 30 years of working with clients, many of whom were retirees, I've noticed that they can very quickly lose mental acuity. Having various retirement accounts might have made sense at some point, but after a few years, having multiple accounts and multiple statements and tax forms can become overwhelming or cumbersome to deal with.

Another important decision to consider is how much fixed income you need versus assets that can potentially grow to outpace inflation. If you have fixed income from Social Security and a pension, consider keeping your retirement account in liquid investments that you can access as needed. You'll appreciate having the flexibility to take a large withdrawal once in a while, perhaps to rent a beach house for a week or to buy a new car. What if you have a medical crisis that costs tens of thousands of dollars?

By keeping your retirement account liquid, you—or your financial advisor—can choose how to invest it and take distributions from one fund or another depending on market conditions.

Be wary of annuity salespeople who might instill fear and tempt you with guarantees. Annuities are typically expensive, are complicated, and do not offer you additional tax benefits compared with an IRA. They lock up your money for years and can come with stiff penalties should you change your mind or need to access more than the allotted amount in a given year.

Have you done your retirement budget? It's important to prepare as accurate a retirement budget as you can. It's your financial road map, and an accurate budget, just like a reliable road map, will help you get to your destination on time.

A good retirement budget can give you the confidence to retire with minimal financial stress while protecting against the risk that you could last longer than your money will.

By the time you're close to retiring, you should have a good sense of what your monthly and annual expenses will be. Just look closely at your current expenses and adjust them to take into account any changes in lifestyle.

Maybe you'll have paid off your mortgage. You'll spend less on work-related costs, such as clothing and daily transportation. But maybe that has already happened as we've adjusted to more work from home in recent years.

Perhaps you'll spend more on entertainment and travel, at least in the early years of retirement. Make those adjustments.

Tally all your expenses, and then do the same for your various sources of income such as Social Security (remember to deduct your Medicare B premiums) and pension. Then reduce further to account for tax withholding. Is there a gap? How will you make it up?

For example, if your total annual expenses are $100,000, and your combined income from Social Security benefits and government pension adds up to $80,000 after taxes, where will you find the remaining $20,000? Perhaps from an IRA or a regular brokerage account. Maybe you have a rental property already generating that income.

Work out a realistic plan that is as detailed and accurate as possible before you retire, and then monitor it regularly. If there's a mismatch between expenses and income, and you're spending down your assets faster than looks sustainable, review everything and make adjustments as necessary. Be ready to stop by the roadside and look at that map before you risk going too far off course.

Do you have a plan B? What if things go awry? Maybe you've done as good a job of planning as you could have, but something unexpected occurs. Perhaps the stock market tumbles just as you're about to retire, and your nest egg isn't as large as you thought it would be. It's wise to evaluate your options and retain contacts with those in your industry. Perhaps you decide you'd like to continue some sort of work. You may be exhausted from your day-to-day career but find that working a couple of days a week as an independent contractor or a substitute teacher gives you some extra income and personal satisfaction.

Always have a plan B or be ready to reevaluate and adapt. That's a great time to work with a trusted financial advisor and explore various scenarios. For example, as an independent contractor or a part-time employee, you may have opportunities to continue to save for retirement. We have many clients who use this extra income to fund Roth IRAs for themselves and their retired spouse! The key is to be aware and respond to unforeseen events sooner rather than later, and if you're even a little concerned, consider "gliding" into retirement by working a couple of days a week.

HOW YOU CAN BENEFIT FROM WORKING
WITH A FINANCIAL ADVISOR

Throughout this book, I've made a few references to the value of working with a financial advisor or, more specifically, a fiduciary financial advisor. I'd like to revisit that here.

First, not everyone wants to or perhaps even needs to work with a financial advisor. Some people's needs are simpler than others. And some people—although not that many in my opinion—are truly capable of making all the important financial decisions in life without professional guidance.

Overall, just three in 10 Americans use a financial advisor, according to the National Association of Plan Advisors. Those most likely to do so have incomes of $100,000 or more and are college graduates. Interestingly, men (35 percent) are more likely to use a financial advisor than women (25 percent).

In a previous book, *Middle-Class Millionaire Women*, I made the case for why more women could benefit from the professional guidance of an independent, trusted professional. So I find that statistic interesting.

There's a strong general case to be made for the benefit of working with a financial professional. To me, that goes beyond your gender or level of income.

Just as you see a professional health provider rather than winging it and self-diagnosing things like cancer or heart disease, isn't your financial health as important as your physical health? I think there's too much at stake to be making mistakes with either one.

It's important to work with someone who has the expertise that comes with a respected professional designation, such as a Certified Financial Planner™. It's also very important that you work with someone whom you truly can trust, a fiduciary advisor. The word "fiduciary" means that the financial advisor has a legal as well as a moral obligation to put your needs first. One of the key questions to ask any financial advisor is, "Are you a fiduciary?"

Rather than being motivated to sell you products and earn a commission, focusing on a transactional relationship that may or may not be in your best interest, a fiduciary financial advisor should be there to form a long-term relationship with you and help you with any financial issues that you face throughout your life.

Additionally, for government employees, there are complex and confusing rules and regulations that are unique to government benefits. So it can be additionally helpful for government employees and retirees to seek unbiased, professional guidance on these issues. But even more than that, it's critical to work with a fiduciary advisor who knows about government retirement benefits.

At Kendall Capital, we are fiduciary advisors who have extensive experience working with clients who are or were employed by the federal, state, or local government. We may not know every answer to every question, but we can help find them out. We can flag important things for you to think about. And we can help you come to the decision that is right for you in your specific situation, something that you can feel comfortable with and that will feel right for you.

We're here to help you reach your goals, with no vested interest other than to help you do well and continue to earn your trust.

YOUR NEXT STEPS

Whether you've read the entire book or skimmed it and skipped ahead, here we are at the end. Now it's up to you. What next steps should you take so that you can take full advantage of your financial deck of cards at this point in your life?

1. Review your current finances. Let's assume that retirement is approaching. You'll want an accurate assessment of all of your finances. That includes your current and projected retirement budget, as discussed earlier. Also, thoughtfully assess your retirement readiness. If you aren't ready to retire just yet, do you have a target date in mind? What must you do to meet that target?

2. Envision your future. Perhaps you've been doing this planning and envisioning for a while. The basic questions to ask yourself include the following: When? Where? Why? What? How? And how much?

When will you retire?
Where will you live?
Why are you retiring? (Are you ready psychologically as well as financially for the change?)
What do you want to do with the rest of your life?
How do you make your future plans and dreams a reality?
How much do you have financially, and how much will you need? (This loops back to your financial readiness.)

3. *Create a to-do list.* You've done the work. You've saved, you've invested, and you've taken advantage of the government deck of cards. It's time to put the last steps into action. Exactly what do you need to do? Talk with your personnel department to finalize a retirement date. Make sure all your benefits are in order. Make the necessary changes, if any, to benefits options for the transition into retirement. What else? Write it down. Make it happen.

4. *Write down a list of questions.* Do you have any remaining unanswered questions? Are they questions that need to be discussed with your spouse or partner? Can they be answered by your personnel representative at work? Or perhaps your financial advisor? Whatever these questions are, identify them and get answers.

5. *Meet with your financial advisor.* This should be a transition-focused meeting. You are about to go through one of life's biggest changes, after all. Use your resources, including your trusted fiduciary financial advisor, who is there for you as an unbiased expert guide or financial coach through life's major events and transitions. Get all of your questions answered, and be open to all possibilities.

In today's world, each of us has the freedom to play our own cards. You can put your own personal stamp on the meaning of "retirement."

Are you ready? Enjoy the ride!

CHAPTER 10
The Many Joys of Government Careers

In closing, for our final chapter, Carol and I want to share why we enjoy working with middle-class millionaire government employees. Both she and I have over 20 years of experience in the investment management industry and could have worked for one of the large financial institutions or brokerage firms. Instead, we chose to work with hardworking individuals and families, many of whom have a calling to help others through their service in our governments at the federal, state, and local levels.

For us, their unique opportunities are like puzzle pieces that we can help them put together in order to visualize their dreams. Some of the greatest rewards we receive are pictures of smiling fathers walking their daughters down the aisle at their weddings or watching our clients' children move their tassel from one side of their cap to the other at graduation. We also get to encourage our clients to dream a little bigger and spend a little more because they had tightened their belts and made the most of their retirement plans.

For us, seeing our clients enjoy the benefits of using various financial planning and investment management tools, unique to government careers, is incredibly gratifying. The following are stories from some of them—their motivations, tribulations, journeys, and descriptions of the work they did, or still do, for various governments. We thank them all for their service, as they, too, had other career options.

PEGGY: FINANCIAL INDEPENDENCE IN HER 90S

Peggy, a Kendall Capital client in her 90s, grew up in the mountains of North Carolina and learned to take care of herself at a very young age. After a few years of running a hotel with her husband, she realized she'd have to make a change, as he wasn't pulling his own weight with the business. She divorced him in the early 1960s and moved to Washington, DC, where she sought better educational and job opportunities. She also had family there.

When she arrived in the nation's capital, she didn't have much money, but she was smart and knew if she could learn some secretarial skills, the federal government would hire her without discrimination. After enrolling at Strayer College and obtaining her secretarial certificate, she was immediately hired. As a young adult, she had volunteered in the Women's Army Corp, so she was familiar with Washington, DC.

"During my 30 years of federal government service, I worked for a variety of departments, and I loved that I continued to serve my country," Peggy said. "I lived on Capitol Hill because it was exciting, and I kept my ears open to listen to politicians discuss current events and propose solutions."

Peggy continued to attend college at night, eventually earning her bachelor's degree in accounting. For her, working for the federal government provided a path to financial security and stimulated her mind. Despite her modest upbringing and her divorce, she was given the opportunity to contribute and serve our nation because she had grit and was willing to learn new skills. To this day, Peggy listens to C-SPAN and keeps tabs on current events. She's proud of herself and her ability to be financially independent in her 90s. She also made sure her mother was well cared for back in North Carolina. Growing up poor, she wasn't lured by material things. Peggy has lived a simple life and was able to save much of her salary, resulting in her ongoing financial security—she's a typical middle-class millionaire.

KATHY: HELPING TO REDUCE HOMELESSNESS

Kathy, a social worker for Montgomery County, Maryland, values the stability of being a government employee over a private sector job. She is also motivated to help the community by working to reduce homelessness.

"I've worked for the county government for more than 20 years," Kathy said. "I feel good about representing the county as a social worker on the front lines helping to find the resources and support for people facing homelessness, mental illness, and addiction. The benefits are generous, both as an active employee and into retirement. I am paid well, and in my position, I doubt I would earn as much working for a nonprofit. I like the structure and support I have working for the county as opposed to going into private practice. As a member of the union, I have many additional benefits and support for equitable compensation and safe working conditions."

KEN: PROTECTING AMERICANS WHO
RELY ON MEDICARE AND MEDICAID

Ken, a health care expert, left his lucrative career as a partner in a DC law firm to apply his skills to help oversee Medicare and protect programs that millions of Americans rely on. He spent the first 26 years of his career as a health care lawyer at two law firms in Washington, DC, including a stint as a partner with a large international law firm. Following his successful run there, as his retirement age drew closer, Ken wondered whether he could move to the public sector for the rest of his career. Many of his former law firm partners and close relatives had served in the US Navy, the US Army, the Marine Corps, the New York Police Department, and the Fire Department of New York. He had never done any of that.

"My decision to give public service a try was driven primarily by my desire to give back a little something to the country that had provided me and my family with so much opportunity and stability. I was also excited about the prospect of practicing law without having to track billable hours!"

Ken spent the final nine-plus years of his career in the Office of Counsel to the Inspector General within the US Department of Health and Human Services. There, he worked with investigators, analysts, and other attorneys from his own office, from other HHS components such as the Centers for

Medicare & Medicaid Services, and from the Department of Justice. Their mission was to oversee the integrity of major federal health care programs, especially Medicare, and to help protect Americans who relied on these programs.

"As a law firm partner, I had often heard good clients who worked hard to comply with applicable laws and regulations complain that they were severely disadvantaged when forced to compete with unscrupulous providers who sometimes pushed through the boundaries of legality. They said that they just wanted to compete on a level playing field. So I was proud to use my legal expertise and experience to try to address that problem. That mission gave me a fulfilling sense of citizenship and pride."

Ken's salary in the government was much lower than his law firm compensation, but it was solid. Moreover, his excellent health insurance benefits had no preexisting condition limitations and could carry over into retirement. In addition, his more predictable work schedule enabled him to take more time off for recreational adventures and to be with family. It's all about trade-offs. This professional path worked extremely well for Ken.

JACK: SCIENTIST HELPING TO
SHARPLY REDUCE POLLUTION

Jack is a scientist with people skills who valued the long-term perspective our government has, compared with the more short-term, profit-driven private sector. He worked for the Office of Oceanic and Atmospheric Research (OAR) within the US National Oceanic and Atmospheric Administration. OAR provides a wide range of support to the other line offices within NOAA as well as to other federal agencies.

"I worked in the Air Resources Laboratory (ARL), which was originally a part of the Weather Bureau," Jack recalled. "My original boss, Dr. Lester Machta, figured out where the Soviets were doing atomic weapons testing. The tools that he developed, coupled with several models developed by smart computer programmers, later became ARL. In the early days, data collection primarily concerned radionuclides. Then, when atmospheric testing ended, much of the data addressed more garden-variety pollutants, such as sulfur, nitrogen, and mercury compounds, as well as agricultural chemicals.

"The basic tools remain the same, whether they were addressing things that could kill you quickly or if they would take 30 or so years to show a harmful impact. I was the ARL Deputy Director from 1990 until I quit in 2017. In my role, I worked with both the modelers and the data gatherers and experimentalists in the lab."

While Jack was working on his master's degree at the University of Virginia, a professor had a contract with NOAA/ARL to help with NOAA's acid rain program. Jack and his university associates were able to source the deposition of sulfur and nitrogen compounds in Bermuda back to power plants in the mainland United States, a breakthrough finding at the time. That experience led to his joining ARL.

"I was tempted to leave ARL many times," Jack said. "The lab was chronically underfunded. I received an offer from a power company to run a number of their weather models, and I was recruited to join the 'dark side' and work with a number of lobbying organizations that wanted to kill federal regulations concerning pollution control. However, I stayed because I believed in the work being done in the lab, I had a great staff of very talented people, and I got to work on cutting-edge science and rub shoulders with leading scientists from all over the world who were wrestling with the same issues. I traveled to Europe frequently and all over North America. It's hard to do this in the private industry, particularly in cool places looking at cutting-edge science.

"Although in the private industry, you can make a lot of money in the right place at the right time if you're any good, the private sector is driven by profit, and when things don't work out, you have to find another job. By its nature, the private sector is rarely focused on very long-term social and environmental issues. In contrast, in government, particularly in the research labs, sometimes you have the luxury to focus on such things, and it can be a lot of fun. In my career, I was able to focus on the energy industry—mostly pollution issues—and was able to follow the sharp decline from 30 million tons of sulfur dioxide emissions down to three or four million tons, which is where we are now. That's a reduction of almost 90 percent. We made a difference!"

In assessing the benefits and drawbacks of working for the federal government versus the private sector, Jack said he "was adequately compensated. Medical and retirement benefits were pretty good. Perhaps I could have done better in industry but probably with less job satisfaction and probably with less stability, even though the federal government has its problems. However, once you get to the position of lab director or higher, pay and benefits are clearly much better outside of the government. Who in the private sector manages tens of thousands of employees and makes less than $200,000 a year? I thoroughly respected the lab directors who were really good at an area of science and directed important areas of research. These people were born to do their line of work, and I believe that most of them were going to do it whether they were paid or not, somewhere and some way."

GLOSSARY

Annuities/Annuitize: An annuity is a financial product in which the annuitant (person buying the annuity) purchases a stream of guaranteed income, typically for life. One way to provide some form of guaranteed income for life is to annuitize some assets, which will provide you income, in addition to Social Security benefits, throughout your life. Annuities can be fixed or variable, deferred or immediate.

Asset allocation: The act of creating a mix of portfolio assets that reflects your individual timeline and risk tolerance, among other factors.

Beneficiary designation: A beneficiary designation is the act of naming the person who will inherit an asset in the event of the account owner's passing.

It is vitally important to name and update designated beneficiaries on any account that could involve the transfer of assets when you die, including any kind of retirement account, company pension, annuity, or life insurance policy.

Catch-up contributions: A catch-up contribution is a type of retirement savings contribution that allows people aged 50 or older to make additional contributions to employer-sponsored retirement accounts, such as 401(b) or 457(b) accounts and individual retirement accounts (IRAs).

COLA: Cost of living adjustments (COLA) are typically made each year on benefits, including Social Security benefits as well as those in the CSRS and FERS government retirement plans.

CSRS: The Civil Service Retirement System (CSRS) is a public pension fund that since 1920 has provided retirement, disability, and survivor benefits for most US federal government civilian employees. It covers employees who were hired before 1984. Federal government employees hired since 1984 are covered by the Federal Employee Retirement System.

Deferred annuity: A deferred annuity is a contract with an insurance company that promises to pay the annuity owner a regular income, or a lump sum, at some future date.

Defined benefit plan: A defined benefit plan is an employer-sponsored retirement plan in which employee benefits are computed using a formula that considers length of employment and salary history, along with other factors.

Defined contribution plan: A defined contribution plan is a retirement plan in which the employee and/or the employer contribute to the employee's individual account under the plan.

Dollar-cost averaging: The practice of investing the same dollar amount at regular time intervals, such as once a month. By buying the same dollar value, you purchase more shares when the price falls and fewer shares when it rises.

Dividends: The regular payment of a designated share of profits by a company to its shareholders on a per-share basis.

Emergency fund: Designated savings that you could draw on in an emergency. It is generally recommended that people should have a large enough emergency fund to pay for at least three to six months' worth of living expenses.

ERISA: The Employee Retirement Income Security Act (ERISA) is a federal law that protects the retirement assets of American workers. It covers a variety of defined benefit and defined contribution retirement plans.

FEGLI: The Federal Employees Group Life Insurance (FEGLI) Program is a group term insurance program that offers a basic benefit plus three optional add-ons.

FEHB: The Federal Employees Health Benefits (FEHB) Program is the largest employer-sponsored health insurance program in the world, covering more than eight million federal employees, retirees, former employees, family members, and former spouses.

FERCCA: FERCCA stands for the Federal Erroneous Retirement Coverage Corrections Act. It addresses the long-term harm to retirement planning created when employees are put in the wrong retirement plan.

FERS: The Federal Employees Retirement System (FERS) is the retirement plan for US federal employees. The plan covers all employees in the executive, judicial, and legislative branches of the federal government. Under FERS, employees receive retirement benefits from three sources: the basic benefit plan, Social Security, and the Thrift Savings Plan (TSP).

Fiduciary: A person who acts on behalf of another person or persons to manage assets. A fiduciary has a legal and ethical responsibility to act in good faith.

GPO: If someone receives a pension from a government job but did not pay Social Security taxes while they had the job, through the Government Pension Offset (GPO) program, the federal government will reduce that person's Social Security spouse, widow, or widower benefits by two-thirds of the amount of their government pension.

High 36: The high-36 method of calculating government pension benefits uses the average of the highest 36 months of basic pay divided by 36. This is generally the last three years of service and is sometimes called high three.

Individual retirement account (IRA): Individual retirement accounts (IRAs) are investment accounts intended for retirement savings. They allow earnings to accumulate on either a tax-deferred basis (traditional IRAs) or a tax-free basis (Roth IRAs). The key difference between a traditional IRA and Roth IRA is that with a traditional IRA, you receive a tax break up front through a tax-deductible contribution, but you pay taxes on withdrawals; and with a Roth IRA, you don't receive a tax break until you withdraw from the account. At that time, as long as certain conditions are met, you pay no taxes on the amount contributed to the Roth IRA or any earnings.

Joint and survivor annuity: A type of immediate annuity that guarantees payments for as long as the annuity owner or the beneficiary lives.

Long-term care insurance: A long-term care insurance policy is designed to cover long-term care needs, services, and support. In other words, it pays for needs arising from a chronic illness or medical condition.

Longevity risk: The risk of outliving your money. It is one of the primary reasons to make sure one has saved sufficiently for retirement.

Matching contribution: A type of contribution that an employer makes to its employees' employer-sponsored retirement plan according to an established formula.

Medicare: A single-payer national health insurance program that covers seniors and is composed of various parts, including hospital insurance, medical insurance, and prescription drug coverage.

Opportunity cost: Opportunity cost is the value of what you give up whenever you make a decision. It is the loss of potential gain had you chosen the alternative. If you spend $50,000 on a car, for example, an opportunity cost might be what that money would earn if you invested it instead.

Required minimum distributions (RMDs): Mandatory withdrawals from an IRA, SIMPLE IRA, SEP IRA, or retirement plan account when you reach age 70.5.

Roth vs. traditional IRAs: See individual retirement account (IRA).

Rule of 72: The rule of 72 is a formula that estimates the number of years it takes to double an investment at a given annual rate of return or interest. For example, at a steady annual return of 8 percent, it would take 9 years to double an investment, but at a 4 percent annual return, it would take 18 years.

Socially responsible investing: Socially responsible investing, or social investment, is any investment strategy that considers both financial return and social and environmental good to bring about social change regarded as positive. It is also known as sustainable, socially conscious, "green," or ethical investing.

For example, a socially responsible fund might avoid industries that negatively affect the environment and its people. However, it might include companies that produce or invest in alcohol, tobacco, gambling, and weapons. In other words, each investment fund defines how it views social responsibility and why it considers a given company socially responsible.

Survivor benefits: Benefits payable to your surviving spouse after you die. For example, if you retire under the Federal Employees Retirement System (FERS), the maximum survivor benefit payable is 50 percent of your unreduced annual benefit.

Tax-deferred accounts: Accounts (typically retirement accounts) in which investment earnings—including interest, dividends, and capital gains—accumulate tax-free until the investor takes distributions.

Thrift Savings Plan (TSP): The TSP is a retirement savings and investment plan for federal employees. It is similar to a private sector 401(k) plan or state 403(b) and other similar plans.

Vesting: Vesting refers to the percentage of an employee's retirement account that they own. While the contributions an employee makes to their plan are always 100 percent vested, the employer's matched contributions are not always automatically vested. An employee might need to have a set number of service years for the matched contributions to be 100 percent vested.

Volatility: Volatility describes the tendency for investments, such as the stock market, to rise or fall. More volatile investments often have a higher potential return, while less volatile investments tend to have lower returns. In a sense, investors are rewarded for accepting volatile investments.

Voluntary Contribution Program: The Voluntary Contribution Program was developed for employees who are part of the Civil Service Retirement System (CSRS). It allows those employees to contribute their own money into an account that can later be used to increase their annuity when they retire.

Windfall Elimination Program (WEP): The WEP is a formula used to adjust Social Security worker benefits for people who receive "noncovered pensions" and qualify for Social Security benefits based on other Social Security–covered earnings.

Yield: Yield refers to how much income an investment generates, apart from the principal. It is commonly used to refer to interest payments an investor receives on a bond or dividend payments on a stock.

ACKNOWLEDGMENTS

Thank you to the many Kendall Capital clients for sharing their stories of being a government employee. This book shares *what* your government benefits are and *how* to embrace, use, and benefit from them. But, it was our clients who shared *why* they worked for various government agencies and the motivations for their service to the greater good. We feel that their warm stories add heart and soul to what, admittedly, can be a dry topic.

Carol and I must also, once again, thank Allan Kunigis for staying focused with us as we wrote, rewrote, and then rewrote this book again. Allan was a pleasure to work with as he helped Carol and me bring this book to fruition.

Lastly, I must acknowledge and appreciate my colleague, Carol Petrov, for her servant heart to help others. As with everything she does, she jumped through hoops to make this book easy to understand for as many people as possible to benefit and enjoy. Her generous spirit is evident on a daily basis as she serves client needs at Kendall Capital, and she poured all her experience and kindness into the words in this book.

—Clark A. Kendall

ABOUT THE AUTHORS

Clark A. Kendall started Kendall Capital in 2005 with a phone, a desk, and the goal to help and serve the Washington, DC, area's middle-class millionaires as a fiduciary advisor. Since then, Kendall Capital has grown tremendously, but his commitment to middle-class millionaires has remained. Clark's success and understanding of this demographic comes from melding 30 years of experience in investment and wealth management with the academic knowledge obtained from the Chartered Financial Analyst® (CFA), Accredited Estate Planner® (AEP®), and CERTIFIED FINANCIAL PLANNER™ (CFP®) programs.

Clark is a former equity seat holder on the New York Stock Exchange (NYSE) and a member of the Washington Society of Chartered Financial Analysts®. He is also an active member in various community organizations, including the Boy Scouts of America, Olney Boys and Girls Community Sports Association, Young Life, Big Brothers Big Sisters of America, and the Universities at Shady Grove mentor program.

Clark is a graduate of James Madison University and holds a Bachelor of Business Administration (BBA) in finance and economics. Clark and his wife of 36 years, Diane, reside in Sandy Spring, Maryland. They are most proud of their four grown children and their growing portfolio of talented grandchildren.

Carol L. Petrov is a CFP® and CPWA® professional with over 20 years of experience as a financial planner and relationship manager. She joined Kendall Capital in 2014, seizing the opportunity to help clients as a fiduciary advisor. She provides comprehensive financial planning services for new and existing clients while managing ongoing client needs. In addition to providing actionable advice, Carol and the team at Kendall Capital strive to provide excellent service that their clients can count on through good markets and bad. She works with estate attorneys and accountants to help their clients enjoy the benefits of comprehensive financial planning.

Carol earned her bachelor's degree from the George Washington University School of Business, received her designation as a CERTIFIED FINANCIAL PLANNER™ in 2012, and received her Certified Private Wealth Advisor® certification in 2021. When not at work, she enjoys volunteering with her local chapters of the Daughters of the American Revolution and League of Women Voters, and cheering on her son at sports.